Wine-Tasters' Logic

Pat Simon was educated in Norfolk and France, returning to the UK to take a degree in Modern Languages at Trinity Hall, Cambridge. Following service with the Royal Artillery and at Field Marshal Montgomery's headquarters from 1940 to 1946, he entered the wine trade in 1948. As director of a number of companies he gained a wealth of experience in all branches of the wine and liqueur trades. In 1966 he became a Master of Wine, making him one of the early recipients of this prestigious title, which he has held now for more than thirty years. He has acted as wine consultant to the UN Food and Agriculture Organisation on the World Bank Co-operative Programme, and has been Chairman of the Education Committee of the Institute of Masters of Wine and a Member of Council of the Wine and Spirit Association. Over the years Pat Simon has written on wine and contributed articles to, amongst others, *Wine* magazine and the *Observer* magazine.

FABER BOOKS ON WINE
Series Editor: Julian Jeffs

Barolo to Valpolicella, The Wines of Northern Italy by Nicolas Belfrage
Bordeaux (new edition) by David Peppercorn
Burgundy (new edition) by Anthony Hanson
Champagne by Maggie McNie
French Country Wines by Rosemary George
Haut-Brion by Asa Briggs
Madeira by Alex Liddell
Port and the Douro by Richard Mayson
Sauternes by Stephen Brook
Sherry (new edition) by Julian Jeffs
The Wild Bunch: Great Wines from Small Producers by Patrick Matthews
The Wines of Alsace by Tom Stevenson
The Wines of California by Stephen Brook
The Wines of Greece by Miles Lambert-Gocs
The Wines of the Loire by Roger Voss
The Wines of New Zealand by Rosemary George
The Wines of the Rhône (new edition) by John Livingstone-Learmonth
The Wines of South Africa by James Seely
The Wines of Spain by Julian Jeffs

WINE-TASTERS' LOGIC

Thinking about Wine –
and Enjoying It

PAT SIMON

faber and faber
LONDON · NEW YORK

First published in 2000
by Faber and Faber Limited
3 Queen Square, London WC1N 3AU
Published in the United States by Faber and Faber, Inc.,
an affiliate of Farrar, Straus and Giroux, New York

Phototypeset by Intype London Ltd
Printed in England by Clays Ltd, St Ives plc

Pat Simon is hereby identified as author
of this work in accordance with Section 77
of the Copyright, Designs and Patents Act 1988

Illustration of International Tasting Glass on page 13
reproduced by permission of the British
Standards Institution

A CIP record for this book
is available from the British Library

ISBN 0–571–20287–X

2 4 6 8 10 9 7 5 3 1

Contents

Figures and Tables

FIGURES

TABLES

I
THINKING ABOUT TASTING

I

Defining and Refining

TASTE

'De gustibus . . . semper disputandum est.'

'Nice' and 'nasty' are two of the earlier words learnt by a child,
and they reflect personal reactions to taste. Taste is one of the
senses, and, when gratified, it gives hedonistic pleasure. But these
natural reactions may become overlaid as we are taught to be
members of society, and learn to adjust to accepted 'good taste'.
We can become conditioned to the surrounding lifestyle.

WINE

Wine is a paradox – a natural product that does not occur spon-
taneously in nature. It is also a perishable product that may be
improved with keeping.

From among the multiplicity of beverages called 'wine', we shall
limit ourselves to those made from the fermented juice of grapes,
the fruit of the grapevine.

GRAPEVINES

Grapevines are perennial plants, and their growth patterns and
type of produce vary widely, according to where they grow, and the
way they are treated. Sexual reproduction results in bunches of
grapes, consisting of individual fruits where pulp, juice and skins
enclose pips (except for seedless varieties), which are the plant's
seeds.

The grapevine will grow in many parts of the world, but – for

3

historical reasons – wine production has (in the past) been limited to recognized 'wine lands'.

WINE-MAKING

Wine-making was probably discovered by chance, long ago, after which wine-making skills developed in each locality from experience.

The basic common factor is to encourage micro-organisms (yeasts) to transform the sugars in the grape juice into alcohol, while discouraging other micro-organisms from changing the alcohol into vinegar, or producing other off-flavours.

WINE-DRINKING

Wine is taken as an everyday beverage in most wine-producing lands, but in other countries it may be regarded as a luxury, to be enjoyed on special occasions.

As a beverage, wine may be judged on its palatability, for its thirst-quenching success, as an aid to digestion, and for the euphoria it engenders.

As a luxury product, it may raise higher expectations, and be savoured rather than simply imbibed.

WINE-TASTING

The ancient Romans judged wine by colour, aroma and taste – by eyes, nose and mouth – and since our anatomy remains much the same, so do we!

Pleasurable emotions may come into the equation, and physical gratification, and, finally, judgement against a scale of values. So the mind, as well as the body, becomes involved.

LOGIC

It is perhaps a reasonable assumption, that if a person can taste something, there ought to be a reason for it. This book will try to test out the hypothesis that there may indeed exist a 'Wine-taster's Logic'.

TO TASTE

In the English language, the verb 'to taste' can be both transitive *and* intransitive. This should alert us to a recurring risk of logical confusion: mixing up the *stimulus* (i.e. whatever it is in the wine that is tickling our taste-buds), and our *perception* of it, and how we react to it.

BASIC TASTES

Most textbooks will tell you that there are four basic tastes – sweet, sour, salt and bitter – and that these are all that the taste-buds (which are the chemical receptors of the mouth) are capable of discerning.

But we must now learn to accept a fifth basic taste. This is recognized by Japanese sake-tasters, who are trained to a high degree of acuity; for example, when they start their training, for the first two days they taste the different kinds of water from which sake is brewed, and only when they can identify them will they start to learn the different styles and qualities of sake.

In sake-tasting they use a fifth term – 'umami' – which is usually translated as 'deliciousness'. It is now defined in the International Standards Organisation (ISO) vocabulary as the taste of mono-sodium glutamate.

SENSATION

The most immediate and obvious sensation when taking wine into the mouth is 'wetness' – so obvious indeed that we never note it. Illogically, we use its antonym 'dryness', but only in contrast to 'sweetness'!

We do however use what I term 'fingertip words', like those that describe running the fingers over a polished surface or sandpaper – 'smooth' or 'rough'. In tasters' terms, this is 'mouth-feel'.

GESTALT

There is another class of words, used in wine-tasting, that do not fall into any of the above groups, but that evoke images or shapes and forms: words like 'broad' or 'thin', 'round' or 'flabby'. These 'shape-words' seem to lie within the ambit of Gestalt Psychology –the study of images, shapes and forms.

SMELL

Here again we have an English verb existing both in transitive and intransitive form, so that the same note of caution must be uttered, warning against confusing the stimulus (i.e. the aroma molecule) and our perception of it, using receptors in the nasal cavity, and interpreting the signals in the brain.

TRANSITIVE – INTRANSITIVE

Conversation between a society lady and Dr Johnson: 'La! Sir. You smell.' 'Madam, you are mistaken. You smell – I stink!'

FLAVOUR

Many of the components that go together to create flavour are not basic tastes, nor mouth-feel, nor Gestalt images. They can effectively be aromas given off by the wine while held in the mouth, and which reach the nasal cavity from the back of the throat.

AFTERTASTE

After the wine has been swallowed (or the sample spat out), sensations may persist from the stimuli, or, sometimes, other sensations may emerge.

TEMPERATURE

The mouth is sensitive to temperature, and a chilled white wine may be gratifying on a hot day. And mulled (heated) wine can be a happy choice in winter.

Some chemicals can create a 'pseudothermal effect' – menthol giving a sensation of coolness, and red pepper (capsaicin) a hotness. So, when we add ginger and spices to our mulled wine, we are using the pseudothermal effect to accentuate the warmth of the drink.

HEARING

This sense rarely has any role in wine-tasting, although the pop of a champagne cork might have a Pavlovian effect, and give advance warning of seeing bubbles in the glass.

Some wine waiters used to take delight in drawing the cork sharply from a bottle of still wine, again producing a popping sound. This is to be deprecated in an old wine, since the piston effect can create a vacuum in the neck of the bottle, drawing volatile substances to the surface, and assembling them in the portion of wine poured into the host's glass. Such concentrated essence of 'bottle-stink' might well lead the unadvised to utter the ominous word 'corked'. One of the advantages of decanting an old wine is to let any slight traces of bottle-stink 'breathe' out of the wine, and allow the true bouquet to develop.

SEEING

Many years ago I took part in a radio programme on wine-tasting, during which Robin Don produced the Delphic phrase that 'in a blind tasting, a glance at the label is worth twenty years of experience'.

One needs to learn to assemble all available visual clues before using the other senses. For example, a lead capsule (now banned) will indicate an old wine, while plastic capsules are used on run-of-the-mill wines; screw-caps are associated with 'cheap-and-cheerful' drinks, but they are now coming more up-market as a precaution against 'corkiness'.

A low level of wine down the neck or into the shoulder of the bottle suggests longish maturing, but, if associated with seepage, may warn of unsatisfactory storage at some time in the past, or of a dubious cork.

Wines are best stored at an even temperature, since a rise in temperature will cause the wine to expand, and force its way past the cork, while contraction caused by a drop in temperature can draw air into the bottle, with extra oxygenation and risk of premature ageing.

The shape and colour of the bottle may also have their significance. Rhine wines were to be found in brown bottles, and Moselles in green ones. The 'punt' or indentation in the bottom of a bottle may be a relic from the days when bottles were hand-blown, and the bottom had to be pushed in with a 'punty-rod', so that the bottle could stand upright, and did not need to be encased in straw raffia like a Chianti *fiasco*. But when you are decanting an old wine, you may find that the punt has its practical use in concentrating the deposit, while the square shoulders of a claret or port bottle help to trap the deposit as the bottle is gently tilted. Hocks, Moselles and sherries, which generally do not need decanting, are normally in bottles without any punt indentation.

The colour of the bottle may also have its practical purpose. Red wines, traditionally needing longer storage, were put into dark bottles to help protect them from the effects of light, which can cause accelerated ageing. Different colours – greens, browns and blues – may have originated from trace elements in the sand or soda from which the glass was made, but their uses have become either hallowed by time, or seized upon for modern marketing.

Another visual indicator is the way in which a wine flows down the walls of the glass after it has been swirled around. It is usually agreed that these 'teardrops' or 'church windows' can be a sign of quality, but opinion seems to be divided as to how it should be interpreted. Some think that it is linked to the viscosity of a rich wine, or to the presence of natural glycerine resulting from slow or cool fermentation – the glycerine being a by-product of the phosphorilization stage. Now, a link is suggested to the presence of higher alcohol, giving different surface tensions.

LOOKING AT THE COLOUR OF WINE

The majority of grapes have white juice, regardless of the colour of their skins. There are exceptions, such as Gamay Fréaux, or Vranac from Montenegro, the Alicante-Bouschet and its Teinturier cousins, all with red juice and pulp. But white juice means that it is possible to make white wine from red grapes (as in Champagne) by separating the juice rapidly from the skins. The colour of these grapes lies just under the skins.

Short contact with the grape-skins will create a pink or rosé wine, while longer contact is needed for red wines. So we can envisage a continuum of colour development, from white, through deepening shades of pink and red, to a deep red that verges on black, paralleling a wine-making time-scale.

Gardeners know that acid soil produces blue flowers on hydrangeas, while alkaline ground can change them towards pink. Higher acidities in wine can produce a bluish tint in young wines, making white wines greenish and red wines purple; maturity (and oxidation) introduces yellower notes, so that white wines can take on golden tones, while red wines can become brick-red, or – in extreme cases – brown.

NOSING

It is sometimes helpful to make a slight pause when approaching one's nose to the glass: the French use the word *'montant'* to describe how certain wines come up out of the glass to meet you. In dry white Bordeaux wines this may be associated with a higher degree of alcohol (say, 13 per cent alcohol by volume (abv) or more, compared with 12 per cent or 12.5 per cent). But this cannot be the case with the fragrance coming up from a glass of Moselle, with its modest 8 per cent to 10 per cent of alcohol.

Much of wine-tasting is in effect a process of 'compare and contrast'. So it may be illuminating to find what comes to the nose, before swirling the wine around in the glass to increase the surface of liquid exposed to the air.

ACUITY

Musicians with 'perfect pitch' may be relatively rare, but they certainly exist; when a note is played to them unseen, they can immediately say what note it is (i.e. its pitch in the gamut of sounds).

At school I shared a study with a chap named Marshall, who had a photographic memory. When reading a novel, he would scan a page at a time, and take in the gist of it; though when he was studying a subject, he would con only a paragraph at a time, and commit it to memory, to be retrieved at will.

I can imagine that tasters may exist with similar talents, although I have not met anyone so far claiming such infallibility in the wine trade. But expert tasters in other fields have told me about trained assessors working on their tasting panels who have developed remarkable sensory facility in identifying faults in products which they were constantly tasting on a daily basis.

While training in Bordeaux, and trying desperately to discover how on earth one might learn to distinguish one wine district from another, I asked my French cousin whether anyone could identify a wine on blind tasting. His reply was that he had known three men who could do this, but that they were not wine-buyers nor principals of shipping firms. They were the *Maîtres de Chai* of large *négociant* cellars, whose job it was to taste every cask that entered the premises, to ensure that it was what it purported to be and was free from fault or taint. After many decades of doing this, they seemed able to know (intuitively) what every wine ought to be like. Of course, these would only be the wines that they handled; a *bordelais* scarcely acknowledged the existence of burgundy, and seldom, if ever, drank a German wine. In pre-war France I came across port, not as an after-dinner drink, but at a tea-party, when you would be offered '*thé ou porto?*'

FLAVOUR DYNAMICS

Flavour dynamics depends on the observation that certain tastes may be slight, or evanescent, while others may be intense, or persistent. It also depends on the fact that a large part of what we term 'flavour' is effectively aroma distilling off at mouth-temperature, rising through the back of the throat, and being perceived in the nasal cavity.

Tasters have always recognized that, after spitting out the wine, the aromatic flavour continues with a certain intensity, to drop suddenly, and then tail away gently.

The fairly new concept is to time the persistence of aromatic intensity (p.a.i.) in seconds, and to record it in units called 'caudalies' (i.e. 'tail-units'). See Figure 1.

Figure 1
Schematic illustration of variations in intensity of aroma

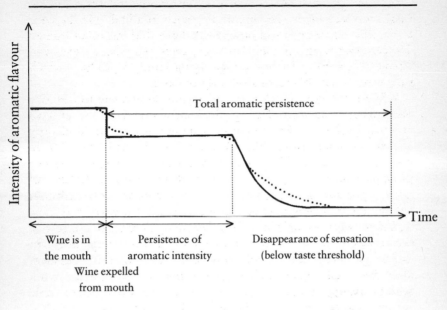

NOTE The hypothesis is that wines of equal repute in the hierarchies will show similar caudalies, even though they may come from different regions or countries. A provisional classification is proposed, in five categories:

	Caudalies
1st	12+
2nd	10–12
3rd	7–9
4th	4–6
5th	0–3

2

Theorizing

WINE IN THE WINEGLASS

Many people would agree that Champagne can be appreciated very differently in the tall slim *'flute'* glass, compared with the shallow open *'coupe'*.

The widely accepted 'International Tasting Glass' (see Figure 2) was originally evolved following a series of experiments in the 1950s by Jules Chauvet, a wine-grower in La Chapelle-de-Guinchay in Beaujolais, and a highly respected wine-taster. His work was based on the hypothesis that surface-to-volume ratios could influence the aroma and flavour of wine.

He placed wines in a variety of containers – such as a flat petri dish, giving maximum surface to minimum volume, as well as different-shaped glasses – and recorded his impressions. He even got a glass-blower to make him a glass nose-piece, that he could fit over his nose and then dip the other end into the wine, so that he was always sniffing a standard measured wine surface. When the International Tasting Glass is correctly filled, the wine forms a liquid hemisphere, giving a surface-to-volume ratio of:

$$\pi r^2 : \frac{2\pi r^3}{3}$$

THE SURFACE-TENSION THEORY

From his observations during this series of experiments, Jules Chauvet gained the impression that aromas arose from the surface of the wine sequentially, or maybe, that they seemed to be *perceived*

Figure 2
The International Tasting Glass

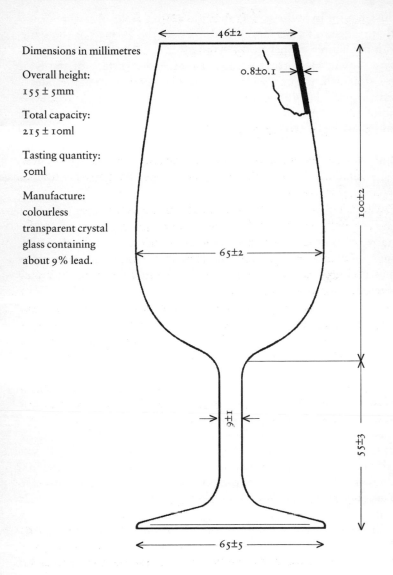

Dimensions in millimetres

Overall height:
155 ± 5mm

Total capacity:
215 ± 10ml

Tasting quantity:
50ml

Manufacture:
colourless
transparent crystal
glass containing
about 9% lead.

46±2

0.8±0.1

100±2

65±2

9±1

55±3

65±5

sequentially by the wine-taster. The sequence in which he usually observed the different types of aroma was as follows:

Flower – fruit – spice – herbs – vegetal – soil notes

The Chauvet hypothesis was that the aroma molecules were generally arranged in a hierarchy of layers on the surface of the wine, with the lighter 'higher notes' at the top, and the deeper soil notes lower down. He further surmised that if the surface of the wine was stretched, the coarser notes could escape and predominate.

It might be helpful at this point if we could elaborate a little on the idea of a 'gamut of aromas'; this is an image borrowed from music, and it is widely accepted in the perfumery world. As an example, one might say that menthol is the same note as garden mint, but an octave higher, or that cinnamon is a similar note to mace, which is an octave lower than cinnamon.

TASTE-VIN

Many years ago, when I was made a 'Vigneron d'Honneur de Saint-Vincent' (resulting from some writing that I had done about the wines of South Burgundy), I was presented with a silver-plated wine-taster, on a ribbon to hang round my neck. In those days, most Burgundian wine-tasters carried their own wine-tasting cups round with them, wrapped in wash-leather. This was understandable when you saw the ill-assorted collection of grubby tumblers and other glasses available in the average wine cellar. I had similarly been in the habit of bringing my usual tasting glasses from England, and carrying one wrapped in a clean handkerchief.

During the ceremony, the Maître-Vigneron of the Confrérie explained how the tasting cup was embellished with hollows and bosses, which had a practical purpose: the hollows gave extra depth for assessing the colour of white wines, while the bosses reflected the light to show the colour and brilliance of the red wines (see Figure 3). In spite of this new knowledge, I continued to use my tasting glasses, since I seemed unable to taste properly with the *taste-vin* – I kept dipping my nose into the wine.

Littré's monumental French dictionary does not use this '*taste-vin*' spelling, but gives it as '*tâte-vin*', and derives the word '*tâter*' (to feel) from Provençal, Spanish and Arabic origins, so maybe I

Figure 3
A *taste-vin*

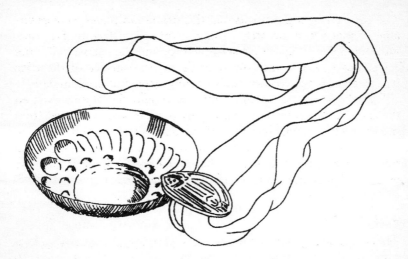

was traditionally feeling the wine with the tip of my nose. On the other hand, Littré quotes from the fifteenth century: '*Comme un bon tasteur du vin . . . après avoir gousté d'un hypocras ou d'un bon vin pineau.*'

This has led me to think again about wine tasting, and to wonder whereabouts most of it takes place. I have often thought that many wine-tasters seem to work with something of a sipping action in the front of the mouth, and then bring the wine into the middle of the mouth, whereas beer-drinkers seem to derive their taste sensations more at the back of the throat.

3

Measuring

YARDSTICKS AND BENCHMARKS

By analogy to mensuration and surveying, benchmarks establish the eminence of a location, while yardsticks are used to measure relative values against a predetermined scale.

Early in my career, I had the great pleasure of drinking 1921 Château Cheval Blanc, and, a bit later, 1929 Château d'Yquem. These are still my benchmarks for claret and sauternes. It is important for the serious taster, once in a while, to drink a superlative wine, at its peak of development. Preferably this should be with a congenial companion, versed in food and wine, and capable of sharing and enhancing the memorable occasion.

Many benchmarks can retain their eminence over the centuries. I like to imagine a medieval inhabitant of Gevrey deciding to plant a new vineyard, and producing wine of such excellence that 'Bert's Field' – Le Champ d'Bertin – became a byword. Not only did neighbouring vineyards – Charmes, Latricières, Mazys, La Chapelle, Griottes, Mazoyères, even the older Clos de Bèze – claim reflected glory from propinquity by adding -Chambertin to their names, but the village did likewise, becoming Gevrey-Chambertin (in 1847).

When Robert Parker or Clive Coates publish the results of their tasting sessions, they are usually 'yardsticking' – Parker on a scale of 50 to 100 (since no American teacher would dare to mark a pupil at less than 50, it seems), and Coates on a scale of 20. Both of them are yardsticking against a presumed (and unstated) benchmark at the top of the scale.

The wine-brokers of Bordeaux, who drew up the 1855 Classification of the Bordeaux châteaux, were yardsticking to a different pattern. They were recording what had emerged from the trends of market prices during past years, and as they operated in a society with clear class distinctions, it was a classification. The top five classes would presumably provide a range of choice for the nobility and gentry, while *crus exceptionnels, crus bourgeois supérieurs* and *crus bourgeois* would suit the middle classes, and the *vins artisans* were for the skilled craftsmen and tradesmen. Peasants would have to make do with the remainder.

LESS IS MORE

> 'I rather like bad wine,' said Mr. Mountchesney;
> 'one gets so bored with good wine.'
> (Benjamin Disraeli: *Sybil*, bk i).

Novice wine-tasters have traditionally been recommended to 'Always drink above what you can afford' (which may seem profitable advice from a wine merchant's point of view); in contrast, maybe we should see what can be learnt from lesser wines. Such wines may be criticised by cognoscenti as being too 'one-dimensional'. Yet this very simplicity can make it easier for the tyro to grasp the wine's essential characteristics.

Next, if we are thinking of wines against scales of values, with a benchmark wine at the top of each gamut, we do not want to have to taste really dreadful wines to put at the bottom of the scale. Instead, let us have a simple drinkable wine to start the comparisons. For example, American 'jug wines' have been described as 'having no vices, and no virtues except drinkability'.

Again, in his book *Alsace and its Wine Gardens*, Fritz Hallgarten gives a menu of the Confrérie de St Étienne:

Sylvaner 1951
Soupe à l'oignon
Brochet de l'Ill Riesling 1949
Sylvaner 1951
Jambon en croûte Tokay 1949
Sylvaner 1951
Fromage des Vosges Gewürztraminer 1949
Sylvaner 1951
Amuse-bouche Tokay 1949

After each course, when the accompanying wine has been finished, and before going up the ladder of richer food and richer wine, a sip of the 'apéritif', of a fresh, light and agreeable Sylvaner, is taken, as a *rince-gueule* – a mouthwash.

4

Analysing

MOUTHING

The mouth is quite a large organ, with many features of significance for wine-tasting. The salivary glands are there to moisten the food, and start the digestive process with the enzyme ptyalin transforming starch to sugars. For the wine-taster it has a slight snag; ptyalin needs an alkaline environment to operate, and wine is acid, so when we take a mouthful of wine the mouth experiences the gustatory equivalent of a culture shock. Because of this, my French cousin used to say that the first wine in a tasting is usually lost.

When I had my first Science lesson, we were given a piece of litmus paper, which we dipped into a solution: if it turned red it was acid, and if blue, alkaline (basic), and if it stayed purple we should know it was neutral (i.e. plain water). We next added some 'acid' to water, and checked, after which we added some 'base' or 'alkaline' chemical to fresh water, and double-checked.

This lesson gave me a workable image that I could live with when I was sent to a Bordeaux laboratory to learn classical wine analysis. I discovered the acidity of my wine sample by titration, dripping a standard alkaline solution from a graduated burette into a measured quantity of wine, until a chemical 'indicator' changed colour. Alkalinity can cancel acidity (as so many stomach remedies repeat). I then looked up the reading on the burette against a set of tables, and recorded the result as grams of acidity per litre of wine (gms/l).

At that laboratory I was put through a pretty stringent tasting discipline. I was required to taste every sample that came in, write down what I thought the analysis figures would be – alcohol, total acidity, volatile acidity, sulphur dioxide, residual sugar – then do the analysis and see how *wrong* I was. At the end of the fortnight I was *not* so wrong; in fact at times my accuracy was close to experimental errors in the analysis.

THE ORAL ACID TEST

I am not at all sure how I did some of it, but as far as total acidity is concerned I suspect that I calibrated my mouth to estimate in time-lapse terms how long the saliva took to neutralize the wine's acidity – in other words, classical titration.

But I had to adjust my thinking about acidity to try to cope with a different way of measuring acidity. Previously I had visualized putting a quantity of certain chemical molecules into water and creating an 'alkaline' solution, or putting different molecules into another lot of water to make it 'acid'. I found that I now had to cope with the pH of wine; I understood this to mean measuring the electrical potential of the concentration of hydrogen ions in a given solution.

Instead of visualizing neatly packaged molecules, labelled with chemical names, floating in the liquid, I had to envisage electrically charged particles floating (or whizzing about) in the liquid, and creating the effect. Some of them might well be akin to those rebellious-sounding 'free radicals' that I had heard about.

Here was a scale, with 7 in the middle indicating the neutrality of pure water, figures above 7 being alkaline, and less than 7 being acid. Confusingly, this meant that the lowest pH numbers related to what I had always thought of as the highest acidities!

However, these two ways of measuring allow us to assess the total quantity of acidity (by titration), and the relative 'acidness' of its ingredients (by pH). For the medieval alchemists, the strongest acid was 'acqua regia' – a mixture of nitric and hydrochloric acid, so strong that it could dissolve gold; fortunately it does not occur in wine. However, I personally came across it during my wine-training; working in the cellars with red wine that had stained my hands blue-black, which soap and water would not budge. I was embarrassed to be dating girls with my hands in that state, so a friend suggested that I go to the pharmacy and get ultra-dilute nitro-hydrochloric acid (used to treat certain stomach complaints), rub it over my hands, and rinse off with water. It certainly worked, and my hands became acceptable, if not lily-white. What he had failed to warn me about were the acute protests from the many minor cuts and abrasions garnered during cellar work.

Similar chemical reactions were called into play when a wine waiter accidentally poured red wine over my tie. He immediately led me to the washroom, poured white wine over the tie to wash the red wine colour out, and then poured on water to rinse out the white wine. The tie survived. If he had used soap, the alkaline in the soap would have changed the red colour to blue (as had happened to my hands) and that colour would have become fixed.

I am still far from clear *how* the mouth senses acidity. The books which tell us of the four basic tastes imply that some of the taste-buds are receptors for acidity, but they do not seem to agree where they are situated nor how they work. I seem to recall that some suggest the tip of the tongue, and others, along the side of the tongue. I personally have never been aware of sensing acidity in this way.

On the other hand, what does ring a bell with me is the reply given when some people are asked to suck a raw lemon and they exclaim: 'Oh no! the thought sets my teeth on edge!' I find that I get a sensation of some of the stronger or sharper acids in wine at the back of my front teeth, or the front of my hard palate. So I begin to wonder whether it might have little to do with chemical receptors, and something to do with nerve-endings responding to electrical charges?

The most likely wine acid to be involved in the 'teeth-on-edge' effect is malic – the green-apple acid. The main grape acid – tartaric – seems to evoke responses more in the middle of my mouth. Needless to say, I have never carried out any controlled experiments on this, and even that would not imply that results from any other individual would necessarily be the same. Nevertheless, self-observation is a necessary discipline for any serious taster.

ALCOHOL IN THE MOUTH

I have a much clearer idea how I estimate the alcohol content of a wine. It is a trick requiring private practice, since early attempts usually result in explosive choking fits, embarrassing for the practitioner, even if amusing for an onlooker.

If you take a small quantity of wine and let it rest on your tongue, you may find that the alcohol creates a slight sense of warmth, similar to the warming (rubefiant) effect of an alcohol rub.

The next stage is to purse your lips as for whistling and draw breath in through the lips, so that a jet-stream passes over the tongue to pick up alcohol vapour. If the lips and tongue are correctly positioned, this alcoholized air-stream should impinge on the back of the soft palate and the epiglottis, with a cooling effect, like putting cologne on a heated brow and fanning it.

The theory behind this procedure is that a greater alcohol content increases each of the effects, and thus increases the temperature gradient. It is assumed that there may be a linear relationship between the alcohol content and the apparent temperature gradient, within the limits of the particular type of wine being studied. The mind must then persuade the mouth to allow itself to be calibrated.

I have found that I have often been able to turn in quite respectable results with the wines of Bordeaux and the Loire, and to a lesser degree, Burgundy; in other areas, results have been erratic, particularly the New World wines. Probably I was better at 'tuning-up' at an earlier age, when I was working intensively on French wines.

SWEET AND SALT

As wine tasters, we need not spend too much time seeking out how to taste 'salt' – it is a rarity in wine terms. Apart from the salty tang of Manzanilla sherry, the only other wines I can recall with this taste are the thin acid wines from the spindrift-washed vineyards of the Isle de Ré and the Isle d'Oléron off the Atlantic coast of the Cognac region. These are distilled into the more ordinary qualities of Cognac.

Sweetness is met far more frequently in wine, and we are probably better equipped for judging it. Every time we answer the question 'One lump or two?' we are assessing our expectations of sweetness.

BITTER

We might well be likely to reject a 'bitter' wine, while welcoming the idea of a pint of bitter beer. This may not however be a true comparison, because bitter beer gains its character from hop resins, while bitterness in foods is characterized in the ISO vocabulary by the tannins of the kaki fruit or persimmon.

In wines, tannins (or anthocyanins, as they are now termed) are important in a number of ways, including colour changes that we have already looked at briefly. We shall need to return to tannins repeatedly, as we explore their roles in wine-making and the maturing of wines, and any tricks that they may demand in the sensory analysis of their influence.

AROMAS IN THE MOUTH

We have already briefly touched on the fact that aroma molecules can reach the nose receptors from wine held in the mouth. We can use this information in a number of ways, for 'compare and contrast', and also as part of our training routine.

Firstly, it might be helpful if we were to think of this as 'fractional distillation'. When we were nosing the wine in the glass, the liquid may be anything between cellar temperature and room temperature – between (say) 55°F and 70°F. In the mouth, the wine will be warmed to somewhere between 95°F and 98.5°F. We now need to compare the aroma perception from the mouth with our recollection of those perceived by nosing from the glass.

If we should find difficulty in recalling all the aroma notes nosed from the glass, we can always go back to nosing, and then re-taste, until we have identified all similarities and differences. In so doing, we may well find that we are training our short-term sensory memory.

We can moreover manage another 'compare and contrast' in the mouth, by drawing air in, and bubbling it through the mouthful of wine. This creates more air-to-liquid interfaces, similar to what we were doing when we swirled the wine round in the glass.

5
Intellectual/Emotional Interlude

In the Middle Ages, the learned Doctors of the Sorbonne disputed by syllogisms the relative merits of Champagne and Burgundy wines. And Volnay was categorized as *'vin . . . nourissant et théologique'* (nourishing and theological wine).

I have long hankered after putting on a musical wine-tasting, with Mozartian Moselles, Brahmsian Burgundies, Claret with Bach, and a rich luscious Barsac accompanying the slow movement of the Bruch Violin Concerto.

I regret that wine-lovers no longer have drinking songs, which now seem to be associated with lager-louts. I wish we could echo the Elizabethan comedy, *A Mad World, My Masters* (Thomas Middleton, 1608), and sing:

> O for a bowl of fat canary
> Rich Aristippus, sparkling sherry!

At the risk of being politically incorrect, I still note certain vigorous wines as being 'masculine', and subtle gentler wines as 'feminine'. And I hang on to the German quotation, strangely attributed to Martin Luther:

> *Alter Wein und junge Weiber sind die beste Zeitvertreiber.*
> (Old wine and young women are the best pastimes.)

Or the alternative version, scribed on to a window:

> *Wer liebt nicht Wein, Weib und Gesang*
> *Bleibt ein Narr sein Leben lang*
> (He who loves not wine, women and song,
> Remains a fool his whole life long.)

MUSCAT/MUSCATEL

One of the most popular wines in the UK in the 1950s and 1960s was a sparkling Saumur muscatel called Golden Guinea. In those politically incorrect days it was reckoned to be a 'ladies' wine'; I recall it as a well-made wine, not to be sneered at. But then people still remembered sugar rationing, and medium-sweet or sweet wines were far more widely drunk than they are now.

But since those days I have begun to wonder whether the concept of 'ladies' wines' was based solely on sweetness, or whether another factor might have been involved. And my thoughts went back to the time (towards the end of the war) when I shared an office at Field Marshal Montgomery's HQ with Simon Field, who had been a perfumer in civil life. Whenever there was a slack moment, he used to expound his ideas about how perfumes worked in reality, as a sexual attractant.

He started with a rather unattractive description about the role of perspiration, and how it could be degraded by bacteria to produce a disgustingly sweaty stench. Ideally, it could be pleasant-smelling, and attractive to the opposite sex. Diane de Poitiers was supposed to have had a most delightful natural skin-perfume, and it was said that H.G. Wells's skin smelt of honey. I suppose Simon was describing what are now known as pheromones.

Simon then went on to propose the idea that physically active people who did not wash too often produced plenty of these sexual attractants, but that they needed scents with flower-notes (lavender or violets, for example) to cover the heavier degraded perspiration notes, whereas the frequent bathing of the leisured classes removed these pheromones, so that their perfumes needed to be helped with civet or musk (animal notes).

Let me now put forward the suggestion that muscat or muscatel grapes might give masculine animal notes, attractive to women. Would that be carrying Simon Field's ideas to unacceptable extremes?

6

Mind-working

———

TRAINING THE MEMORY

As children, we learn to name and distinguish colours, and in
music, we may be taught to separate and remember the different
tonalities of the instruments of the orchestra. But apart from a few
flowers and fruits – roses and violets, oranges and lemons – our
noses seldom go through such courses of instruction.

So we have a great deal of ground to make up when, as wine-
tasters, we are asked to recall a wine tasted in the past, to compare
it with what is being presented in the glass in front of us. We have
to be prepared to use whatever tricks of memory that we come
across and find useful. When I first started making written tasting
notes, I always recorded 'where, when, and with whom'; with this,
I could sometimes recall an image of the occasion, and use that to
retrieve a smell and a taste. This is a reversal of the process that
many of us may have experienced, when a whiff of perfume can
recreate for us an entire scene.

TRAINING THE IMAGINATION

If *memory* is the process of bringing to mind things that have
occurred in the past, *imagination* consists in creating in the mind
things that might occur in the future, or even things that might
never occur in reality.

In visual terms, we can close our eyes, and see things with our
'mind's eye', or, in poetical terms, with 'that inner eye which is the
bliss of solitude'. Musicians need to be able to read a line of musical

notation, and recreate within their heads the sounds intended by the composer.

A composer, working from scratch, forms in his head ideas of new melodies and sounds, and endeavours, through notation, to communicate these ideas to performers, who will then interpret them to arrive at the imagined wishes of the original musician.

A perfumer, creating a new fragrance, blends his alcohols and essences in a way analogous to the blending of the tonalities of musical instruments by the composer. A wine-maker, taking over a winery, has to decide what kind of wine he wishes to make, subject to the vagaries of the available grapes, and then do his best to achieve it, not only gratifying the nose, but also the palate.

The wine-*drinker* might be like a concert-goer, simply enjoying the richness of the tonalities and the emotions engendered. Whereas the wine-*taster* may be like a critical listener, comparing the ongoing performance against his image of how the work ought to sound.

SLOW-MOTION THINKING

One of the things that particularly confused me when I was first learning to taste was the way all the perceptions seemed to come together in a rush. No sooner was I concentrating on identifying a certain aroma note, than its successor came crowding in on its heels, and the first one seemed to disappear before I could pin it down. Or else, if I managed to catch it in mid-flight, its successor seemed to lose precision and focus.

Jules Chauvet suggested to me that if one could accept (at least in theory) that aromas might be arriving in a time sequence – and *not* all at once – it might be possible for the mind to record them all, and then give one a slow-motion playback. I found that it helped me to trick my mind into playing this kind of game if I thought of the aromas coming off in the kind of hierarchy mentioned earlier, and I would then be able to note their presence or absence from the awaited sequence.

SHORT-TERM AND LONG-TERM MEMORY

In the 1950s or early 1960s, some experimenters indicated that the shunting of information from short-term memory into long-term memory was *not* automatic, and that certain techniques could be more effective than others. They suggested that simple repetition might not be enough, and that reinforcement after ten minutes, with revision after half an hour, could often be more effective. Of course, this is probably what experienced teachers have for years been doing instinctively during a forty-minute lesson period!

Unfortunately, during a busy wine-tasting session, few of us can afford to spend much more than five minutes on any one wine, so we tend to rely on note-taking. Tasting notes must, I assume, represent a type of long-term memory, and the act of writing may indeed be a form of reinforcement of short-term memory.

We cannot assume that the words we use will necessarily mean the same to any other person, and it is therefore a source of gratification and amazement whenever I find that my tasting notes are similar to those taken by another taster whose ability I respect.

Some researchers into long-term memory found that a subject learnt in one language, and then relearnt in another tongue, had synergistic reinforcement far in excess of the expected doubling. There may be other advantages in learning wine terms in more than one language; Rhine and Moselle wines can often be described with German words for which there are no real equivalents in French, and the French – for their part – have words that cannot be directly translated into English. But one should also bear in mind that numbers constitute, in effect, yet another language, and if data can be put in numerical form, this may well constitute a powerful reinforcement of memory. Nowadays, wine labels carry more information than they did in the past, and many New World wines have informative back labels with wine-making and analysis data.

WINE DETECTION

It is paradoxical that 'deduction' – which sounds like subtraction – should be known as 'putting two and two together'. Wine-tasters seem to do this all the time. Let us take a hypothetical red wine:

Colour – deep, medium, lightish? *Medium*
Meniscus rim – purple, red, brownish? *Red*
Deduction thus far: probably neither young nor very old.
But what does that mean in terms of months or years?

Beaujolais develops fast, Pinots are slower, some other grapes take even longer. So we have to use the nose, to see if this will produce any varietal clues. And if there are no new clues from nosing, we might need to hold in our minds a couple of possibilities: *either* it is a neutral variety of grape *or* it might be a combination of grapes with no single variety predominating.

At each stage in the process of elimination, where we subtract the 'less likely' from the 'more probable' – i.e. 'deduction' – we may need to bring in new sensory clues, from the eyes, nose or mouth, to arrive at a balance of probabilities.

THE METHOD

In his *Discours de la Méthode*, René Descartes insists on logical progression from a first principle. His logic is based on the syllogism, with a major and minor premise leading to a conclusion. Consecutive logical steps should lead to sound conclusions.

Descartes was aware, however, that a false premise could wreck the logical structure, and he therefore recommended that the chain of reasoning should be checked by self-evident or intuitive inspection. He asserted that in every group or series there would be a predominant factor, and that all others would be subordinate.

I like to think that if there is such a predominant factor in wine, it might be 'harmony' or 'balance', terms easier to recognize than define.

INTUITIVE TASTING

In wine-tasting, with so many disparate sensory clues, to which we may also need to assign degrees of importance or 'weighting', the possibilities of error are innumerable. Descartes's caveat comes to the fore; we certainly need the intuitive part of the method.

Indeed, I suspect that many (if not most) of our best tasters arrive at their conclusions by intuition, allowing the brain to weigh the manifold sensory clues against a mass of acquired experience.

They can then construct a logical explanation, giving weight to the predominant factors, so that they can remember and record their impressions, add all this to their sum of knowledge, and communicate as necessary to others.

'BANKERS'

The wine-taster may well be asked to identify and comment upon the variety of grape in the wine or wines being tasted. One usually starts a process of elimination by identifying or ruling out the 'bankers', those that are most clearly recognizable, such as Traminer or Gewürztraminer. If one is lucky, one may get a clue on the eyes and the nose. Pinot Noir is not at all easy to vinify, and may not have any great intensity of colour; in this case one can look for varietal clues on the nose, and then one seeks reinforcement or elimination on the palate. If I were to get a whiff of cut grass or new-mown hay on the nose, I would start to think of Cabernet Franc. I would then wonder if it came from Italy, where Cabernet Franc can be found as a single variety; in clarets it is apt to be overshadowed by Cabernet Sauvignon or Merlot. Then my second guess would be a Loire red.

One always hopes for the 'blackcurrant' clue to Cabernet Sauvignon, but it may be missed, due to masking by wood notes or soil character.

TABLE GRAPES AND WINE GRAPES

When we buy a bunch of grapes at the greengrocer's, we expect the bunch to *look* good, for we are seldom allowed to pick off a grape to taste it before buying! As a result, table grapes tend to be harvested a little before maximum maturity, since fully ripe grapes are more at risk of being squashed during transit. We are therefore accustomed to a refreshing acidity, balanced by just enough sweetness. The pink-and-white Cyprus table-grape 'Veriko' can be as crisp and crunchy as a pippin apple. Wine-growers who go for extreme ripeness in order to get maximum alcohol may be sacrificing acidity, and the freshness and crispness that it can give. Some Spanish wines have been transformed by earlier picking.

Wine grapes come in many shapes and sizes, but they can be

expected to have a higher sugar-to-acid ratio. The reason for this is clear, if we remember that most if not all of the sugar will be turned into alcohol, leaving the acidity uncovered in what can be an aggressive form.

Moreover, most of the colour, flavour and aroma components lie just below the grape-skins, rather than in the juice, so that the skin-to-juice ratio acquires much significance. If the grape were a perfect sphere, and ignoring the presence of pulp and pips, the theoretical skin-to-juice ratio would be:

$$4\pi r^2 : \frac{4}{3}\pi r^3$$

The smaller the grape, the greater the influence of the size and number of pips on the surface-to-volume ratio. In the Pouilly-sur-Loire vineyards, my old friend Jacques Foucher showed me, time and again, the greater aroma and character of the old small-berried Blanc Fumé (Sauvignon Blanc) compared with the higher-yielding larger clone that was replacing it.

Table 1
Italian system of production control
example from the Lazio or Latium district

Colour	Wine Name	Grape yield per hectare (tonnes)	Percentage extracted	Hectos per hectare
White	Marino	15	72	108
White	Frascati	13	72	93.6
White	Est! Est!! Est!!!	13	70	91
White	Trebbiano di Aprilia	8	60	48
Red	Merlot di Aprilia	8	65	52
Red	Sangiovese di Aprilia	8	60	48

Italian wine law recognizes these variations in juiciness between different varieties of grapes. Whereas French *appellations* lay down the permitted yields in hectolitres of wine per hectare of vines, the Italian regulations state the yields in quintals of grapes per hectare of vineyard, and then the percentage extraction rate permitted when the grapes are pressed and made into wine. The extraction rate varies according to the variety of vine (see Table 1).

7

Balancing

'FRUIT' AND FRUITY ACIDITY

'Fruit' notes often need a good acidity to bring them out, and with German wines the phrase 'fruity acidity' can be a measure of praise rather than a reproach. It may be linked with the word 'crisp' in the case of white wines, a term probably derived from association with the best English eating apples.

I have earlier mentioned my idea that sensing of acidities might be partly an electrical phenomenon. I had started chasing this particular hare (or wild goose?) when I had noticed that every time I had a tooth filled with an amalgam filling it threw my wine-tasting off balance for a few days. I was then told by a dentist friend that he had been obliged to alter the bridge-work for one of his patients, because a gold clip was touching an amalgam filling, and that each time the patient drank any wine, he got an electric shock in his mouth!

So I put forward my 'electrochemical theory of tasting', which linked these observations with the well-known fact that beer tastes different out of a silver or pewter tankard, compared with a glass, and that it can again be different if served in a pottery 'Stein' or (horrors) in a plastic container.

I had the image of the taster, holding a glass in his hand and bringing it to his lips. In the glass, which was an insulator, was an electrolyte (the wine) which went into his mouth, where there was a metallic contact (the amalgam filling). If the hand, holding the glass, made a circuit through the body to the mouth, could an electrical potential be created? Would the potential be different if the glass were replaced by another material?

In the absence of someone willing to put a potentiometer into my mouth while I carried out a tasting, a group of students from the John Cass College tasted some wines from a variety of containers, but the *ad hoc* experiment did not produce any significant results. After all, differences might be due to an interface effect of the wine molecules in contact with a container of a different material.

DRYNESS AND FRUIT

Although 'fruit' seems to be associated with a balanced acidity, some of the 'Trocken' wines now being produced and promoted in Germany seem to lack fruit, while wines from the same vineyards that have *not* been fermented dead dry, but made with a modicum of residual sugar, seem to be considerably fruitier and more attractive.

Our habit of talking generally about 'sugar' is apt to make us forget that we are dealing with more than one kind of sugar. The sugar that we put into our tea or coffee is sucrose, from sugar cane or sugar beet. The main kind of sugar in grapes is glucose, while fructose (which can also be present) is the main sugar in some other fruits. Glucose and fructose have the same chemical composition, but are mirror images of each other, the one bending polarized light rays to the right, and the other to the left – so that they are dextro-rotary and laevo-rotary respectively. Hence glucose is also known as dextrose, and fructose as laevulose.

Cane and beet sugar can be split or 'inverted' into glucose and fructose under the influence of acids. And this is what happens when wines are 'chaptalized' by the addition of sucrose to make up the deficiency in natural grape sugar during unsatisfactory vintages. It also occurs when sugar syrup and yeast are added to instigate the secondary fermentation for sparkling wines.

RESIDUAL SUGAR

With dry wines, virtually all the original sugars will have been fermented through ('*durchgegoren*' in German) into alcohol. For 'off-dry', medium or sweet wines, a residue of unfermented sugar is needed.

Fermentation can stop naturally when all fermentable sugars have been converted to alcohol. It can also end if the alcoholic strength reaches the limit of tolerance of the strain of yeast involved, causing the cells to dehydrate and collapse. It can therefore be stopped artificially by adding alcohol (fortification) either to the fermenting wine (in the case of port), or even to unfermented grape juice, as in Mistelas or Pineau des Charentes.

Fermentation can be stopped mechanically by sterile filtration, or centrifuging, thus removing the yeasts from the wine. Temperature control – cooling to inactivate the yeasts – or heating (pasteurization) to kill the ferments are other methods available. Sulphur dioxide, and sorbates, are chemical means of yeast control.

From the wine-taster's point of view, some of these practices may be discernible, and others not. The striking of a Swan Vesta match used to be a familiar way of illustrating the smell of gaseous sulphur, but the decline of pipe-smoking and the wider use of lighters now makes this a rarity. Sorbates should be scarcely tasteable, but in excess they may impart a slight acrid note. They take their name from *sorbus* – the mountain ash or rowan – so the inquisitive might try the taste of rowan jelly (a Scottish speciality) as a clue to the sorbate tang.

Centrifuging should not be detectable, and neither should sterile filtration, although a badly prepared filter has been known to impart a 'papery' taste from inadequate washing of the filter sheets after the filter has been made up.

Clumsy pasteurization can certainly impart a 'cooked' taste to wine, and has therefore gone out of fashion. If you come across this taste nowadays, it is more likely to be the result of 'thermovinification'. This is the procedure for red wines when the unfermented grape must is heated and then rapidly cooled again in a continuous process, in order to extract more colour from the red grape-skins. This effectively pasteurizes the wine, after which cultivated yeasts have to be added, to start the fermentation.

Even naturally fully fermented wines may have a gram or two of residual sugar, because there are some less usual sugars, such as arabinose, that are not fermented by wine yeasts, and can help to lessen the acerbity of a dry wine.

UNUSUAL CHÂTEAU-BOTTLING

Shortly after I had returned to London from my training in Bordeaux, I found we had a problem with some very sweet château-bottled Sauternes, which had been shipped earlier. Every bottle contained 'flyers'; these were a natural product, looking like tiny scraps of cotton-wool, which the French called *'voltigeurs'*, because they vaulted up into the wine whenever there was the least disturbance to the bottle. As a result, there was no possibility of pouring out the wine without getting some into the glass. So I wrote to the château, asking their advice, and they replied most helpfully, sending me the design of a 'decanting table', with instructions how to get the wine into clean bottles, leaving the fliers behind. They also sent me a supply of branded corks, capsules and château labels, asking me to re-bottle the wine, since it was virtually impossible to return the wine to France. So I can claim the rare distinction of having carried out château-bottling in our London cellars, for a top Bordeaux château.

I cannot recall seeing 'flyers' in German wines, so I suspect that these flyers may have been due to the presence of dextrins. Some old textbooks explained dextrins as being akin to sugars and starches, and I remember reading that, if washed with alcohol, they produced needle-like structures, visible under the microscope. The top German wines have low alcohol, about 7 or 8 degrees, so any dextrins might remain in solution, whereas the sweet white wines of Bordeaux have much higher alcohol – 13 to 15 degrees or more – which might make dextrins come out of solution as flyers. In the past, fine white Bordeaux wines were often fined and bottled without filtration; dextrins were reckoned to add to the palate-fullness of a wine, and are said to be removed by filtration.

It was about that time that I tried (rather unsuccessfully) to sell another unusual château-bottled Bordeaux wine. Pierre Ginestet, who was then the proprietor of Château Margaux, also owned Château de Tastes, an excellent Sainte-Croix-du-Mont estate across the river from Sauternes, producing sweet white wines. He was putting forward the idea that Bordeaux growers should learn from port shippers, and only sell their products as vintage wines in the best years. At all other times (he proposed) they should blend different vintages together, aiming for a reliable standard product, reflecting the essential style and reputation of the vineyard and château. As a pilot scheme, he produced a non-vintage château-bottled Château de Tastes, which I tried to sell to a dubious English market. It was a delicious wine, based on the light and fresh 1948 vintage, enriched with some of the very full (and almost too heavy) 1945 vintage. In theory, it was just what the market needed; but it took no account of the wine-drinkers' innate conservatism of the time.

ACIDITY BALANCE

Sharpness in a white wine is usually due to the amount and type of acidity in the young wine, and wine-makers have to exercise their skills to try to achieve a harmonious balance. In vintages where the level of acidity is high, they will probably encourage a malolactic fermentation, in which a lactobacillus converts the sharp malic acid into a milder lactic acid. If you taste a wine in cask which is going through this process, you might catch a whiff of yoghurt, since *Lactobacillus bulgaricus* is the archetypal ferment to convert milk into 'live' yoghurt.

In other cases, the vinifier may allow the onset of colder weather to chill the wine so that tartaric acid may crystallize out into the lees, leaving the racked wine less acid. The crystals you may sometimes see in a bottle of white wine are such tartaric crystals, and *not*, as some people think, sugar crystals, though at first glance they look like that. The wine-maker will usually try to stabilize the wine during the maturing process in order to prevent such crystalline fall-out. But if you see these crystals attached to the cork, this may be due to the cork merchant, and not the fault of the wine-maker. The increasing demand for cork stoppers has led to a shortage of top-quality corks, and the more widely available dark-coloured corks with a lot of black 'stomata' channels do not look so attractive, even if perfectly serviceable. A number of cork merchants therefore adopted the practice of bleaching the corks, and filling the stomata holes with cork dust. This apparently harmless subterfuge may however trigger a chemical reaction between the bleaching agent and the tartrates in the wine, leading to crystals on the cork, while traces of cork-dust, squeezed out when the cork is compressed to insert it into the neck of the bottle, can act as nuclei for the start of crystallization in the wine, just as clouds may be 'seeded' to cause rain to fall during droughts.

ALCOHOL/SWEETNESS BALANCE

Although German wines, with their relatively low alcohol content, may rely mainly on acidity/sweetness balances for their harmony, white Bordeaux wines need to have their alcohol/sweetness ratios in balance. This was demonstrated to me during my training, when a sample of well-balanced medium-dry white Graves Supérieure was deliberately modified in the laboratory in a variety of ways, so that I could taste them against the control sample.

When the acidity was raised by adding tartaric acid, the wine tasted definitely drier, and a trifle thinner. It also tasted drier when the alcoholic strength was raised by one degree. But when tartaric *and* alcohol were added, it tasted drier, but definitely fuller-bodied.

When sugar syrup was added to the original wine, to raise the sweetness by 18 grams per litre (approximately equivalent to an extra one degree Baumé) the wine was obviously sweeter, but lacked crispness and vinosity, and when the extra sweetness was doubled, the wine started to taste like sugar-water!

Finally, when the original wine was treated with all three additions, it was a fuller and sweeter wine, with a similar balance to the original.

TRIANGULAR BALANCES

The relationship between alcohol, acidity, and residual sweetness was researched by French tasters, and illustrated by a diagram consisting of concentric triangles, with alcohol, acidity and sweetness respectively at each apex, and the balances and flavour characteristics at various positions along the sides.

But before I had come across this, I had worked out for myself a rule of thumb for Bordeaux white wines, assuming normal acidities. I reckoned that a medium-dry Graves (a standard type shipped to the UK in those days) should have 12 degrees of alcohol by volume, and 14 grams of residual sugar per litre of wine, and would then be harmonious and well balanced enough to survive the tribulations of being shipped in cask, and bottled in the UK without too great a risk of secondary fermentation from stray yeasts.

A medium Graves Supérieures needed 12.5 per cent alcohol to balance 28 grams per litre of sweetness; a Sainte-Croix-du-Mont or ordinary Sauternes required 13 degrees of alcohol to carry 54 grams of sweetness, while Haut Sauternes and Haut Barsac, with 72 grams of sweetness needed 13.5 per cent alcohol for balance and stability. I found that these natural balances were put to the test when I used to import Bordeaux wines in cask, bottle them under bond in the UK, and supply them to a Ship's Stores specialist. These wines were then loaded aboard a variety of ships, not just liners with dedicated wine storage facilities. The wines had to be stable enough to survive more than one journey, with changes in temperature including 'crossing the line' with equatorial heat. Fortunately, these wines were shipped to me by my French cousin, who had a fund of experience from supplying the French navy in Indo-China through the firm's agents in Saïgon. Only experience and good tuition can enable a taster to distinguish a healthy and well-balanced wine from one that is 'fragile' and may fall apart under stress.

Tasters' notations can create a problem in assessing balances, especially if each characteristic is assessed against a scale. Such a procedure might well give highest ratings to a wine where every characteristic has very high scores, in balance with each other, no doubt, but putting a premium on 'blockbusters'. This is apt to leave little scope for elegancies and subtleties.

SAKE-TASTERS' NOTATION

We might get some interesting cross-fertilization from the tasting forms that are used by some sake-tasters. These have to reflect the two main influences on sake quality: the water with which it is brewed, which an expert can identify in a blind tasting, and which thus may be reckoned equivalent to the French concept of 'terroir', and the degree to which the rice grains have been polished.

The outer starch granules of rice appear to impart coarser flavours and aromas, and the more they are polished away, exposing the hard central kernel, the finer the sake end-product. The brewing is carried out by the symbiotic action of a mould, converting starch to sugar, and a *Saccharomyces* yeast turning the sugar to alcohol. When I was being taught the basic elements of sake-tasting, I kept wondering whether dextrins were involved.

Dextrins are part-way between starches and sugars, and, if washed in alcohol, can be seen under the microscope as fine strands. They can give a special palate-character to fine white wines, but they are often removed during filtration. In the days when the great sweet white wines of Bordeaux were only fined with isinglass, and never filtered, dextrins could play their part in the breadth of palate-fullness.

NOBLE ROT

Glycerine is another factor in giving smoothness and flow to sweet wines, since glycerine is produced by the *Botrytis* mould during the noble rot, and is also a by-product of the fermentation process. The French have a phrase to describe how a wine can flow across the tongue to fill the mouth with flavour: they call it '*faire queue de paon*', likening it to the splendour of a peacock spreading its tail to reveal its full iridescent glory. Although glycerine can play its part, I think this effect can be partly a surface-tension phenomenon, aided by some of the higher alcohols.

Apart from concentrating the sugars, and producing glycerine, the noble rot has an influence on the acidity of the wine. The moulds seems to use some of the acids for their nourishment, particularly the malic acid, thereby reducing both the amount of acid, and also its sharpness. But as the grapes shrivel and the juice is concentrated, so the tartaric acidity is concentrated, increasing the 'dry extract' and making the resultant wine fuller.

This concentration of the grape juice can inhibit the start of fermentation, particularly with German Trockenbeerenauslesen. And once started, the fermentation is not easy to maintain, so that these top German wines, though rich and long-lived, may well have as little as 8 or 9 per cent of alcohol by volume, compared with the 13 to 15 per cent of alcohol in a top Sauternes or Barsac.

TOKAY–TOKAJI

The finest Tokay wines from Hungary also rely on the noble rot for their essential quality. Here we may find a different approach to the wine-making technique. In the traditional procedures, the bunches of shrivelled noble grapes were placed in a large wooden tub, the base of which was tilted at an angle of 15°. When it was full of grapes, a tap at the lowest part of the base was opened, and the small quantity of juice that had seeped naturally from the grapes under the weight of the accumulated bunches was collected to make Tokay Essenzia. No attempt was made to ferment it – it was probably useless to try – but grape brandy was added to bring it to the desired strength, and it was then left to mature. It was therefore, in effect, not a fermented wine at all, but a superior form of mistela. (Mistela is a way of making a sweet wine simply by adding alcohol to unfermented grape juice.)

The next stage was to crush the bunches in the tub, releasing the remaining juices. In the days of the Austro-Hungarian empire, this was known as the 'Ausbruch' – the 'breaking-out' of the juice. Meanwhile, the rest of the grape harvest had been picked. Some would be made into dry table wine and labelled 'Szamorodni'. But for better and sweeter qualities, small measuring tubs of the Ausbruch mash would be added to the must, to increase the sweetness remaining after fermentation. After Hungarian independence, the German word 'Ausbruch' was replaced by the Magyar equivalent 'Aszú', and the label shows the number of tubs of Aszú that had been added – '3 Puttonos' or '5 Puttonos', and so on. With the higher numbers, the taster can try to search out the characteristics of the noble rot, which should be increasingly detectable in fine vintages with the higher numbers.

The change of spelling to the Magyar form of Tokaji should eliminate some of the confusions arising from the use of the terms Tokayer or Tokay d'Alsace for the Ruländer or Pinot Gris grapes in Alsace wines. The principal grape in Hungarian Tokay or Tokaji is usually Furmint.

We may find that present-day makers of Tokaji Essencia handle the grapes more like a Trockenbeerenauslese, so that we might only discover the unfermented Essencia in very old bottles.

ANTIBIOTIC WINES?

As we have already noted, *Botrytis* is a mould, as are *Penicillium* and the one from which Aureomycin is prepared. Botryticin can be prepared from *Botrytis* mould, and seems to have an antibiotic action. When King George the Fifth was critically ill, the Royal Doctor, Lord Horder, sent urgent messages to the London wine merchants who held the Royal Warrant, asking for Tokay Essenzia. This was found, and rushed to the Palace, and the King made a remarkable recovery. I would like to believe that the concentration of *Botrytis* by-products in such a wine could well have a curative effect.

In exceptional vintages, the top wines of the Moselle also have '*Edelfäule*' or noble rot, and I believe that medieval stories of miraculous cures, leading to one of the wines being dubbed '*Bernkasteler Doktor*' could likewise have a scientific basis.

Doctors in Cyprus for many years used to prescribe Commandaria for ailing children. It seemed to break the vicious cycle of fretfulness–lack of sleep–lack of appetite–fretfulness, and start recovery with weight gain and growth. Commandaria is a rich dessert wine, which can mature in bottle for may years, but the climate in Cyprus is too dry for the noble rot to be present. Commandaria can be made from both red and white grapes, both of which are sun-dried on mats to concentrate the juice. I seem to recall that it was generally the red version that the Cyprus doctors used to recommend.

8

Tannin-sensing

RED WINES AND WHITE WINES

Although I have never experienced it, I understand that a number of people, when blindfolded, cannot tell red wines from white wines. Maybe they do not move the wine all the way round their mouths when tasting, because my experience is that people can generally sense the tannin content of a wine as a 'rough' or 'furry' sensation inside their cheeks. I am not sure how this occurs, but it seems less obvious if the red wine is being tasted while eating meat, especially red meats. The affinities between proteins and red-wine tannins is apparent when we marinade meat in red wine.

The wine-and-food dictum of 'white wine with fish' seems due to the metallic taste left in the mouth when most white fish is eaten with red wine. I was once told that this can be due to a chemical reaction between phosphates in the fish reacting against traces of iron linked to the colour tannins, but so far I have not found anything about this in the literature. Some fish, however, can be happily accompanied by red wines: lampreys and swordfish go well with claret, as can grilled tuna, while salmon and red mullet can be enjoyed with some lighter red wines, or the fuller and finer dry rosés.

Of course, white wines can have an appreciable tannin content, especially with the fashion for heavily oaked chardonnays. White wines with a relatively high tannin content can also be found among many of the traditionally vinified country wines of Italy, where the growers fermented the white grapes on the skins (as they would the red grapes) to produce robust rustic wines to stand up to olive oil and highly spiced dishes.

WINES WITHOUT WINEPRESSES?

We must however consider whether these dark-yellow white wines, fermented on the skins, tell us of an older wine-making technology? A winepress is a bulky piece of equipment, used only for a short period of the year, not readily affordable by a grower with only a few rows of vines. We should consider that wines were made for hundreds of years, even millennia, before winepresses (as we understand them) were introduced; some of these wines must have been made from white grapes. Ancient wineries have been unearthed and investigated in the Middle East by archaeologists.

Even recently, top-quality unpressed white wines have been made. When super-ripe white grapes were loaded prior to pressing, the weight of grapes would squeeze juice from the most luscious ripe-bursting grapes, and this would be fermented separately as 'Crème de Tête'. Similarly, as we have seen, Tokay Essenzia was made from the free-run juice of botrytized grapes crushed under their own weight in a tub tilted at 15° from the horizontal.

OENOTANNINS

Grape tannins provide the colour of the grape-skins, and this can be transferred to the wine. But they also can provide aroma, flavour and body. Hence, they play a role in the overall balance of the wine.

Grape tannins are to be found under the skins of the grapes, and also in the stalks. It can happen that the grapes are more or less ripe, and just pickable, while the stalks within the bunches are still green. This can lead to a 'stalky' and acrid flavour in the wine, if the stalks are left in contact with the fermenting must. I have always had an instinctive aversion to wines with a 'green' taste, but I have been proved wrong on a number of occasions with red burgundies. The Pinot Noir is a challenging grape to vinify, and the burgundian dictum of *'vin vert, riche bourgogne'* can – in the long run – occasionally transform a harsh 'green' cask wine into a full rich bottle after careful and patient maturing.

In the past, grape-stalks could provide a way of identifying wines, since certain wine-growing areas traditionally de-stalked their red grapes before crushing, while others left the ripe stalks in the vats. At one time, it gave a clue to distinguishing the clarets of St Estèphe from neighbouring Pauillac, since many St Estèphe growers kept the stalks in the vats, whereas most Pauillac growers de-stalked their grapes.

In Champagne, both red and white grapes are normally left on the stalks, in the bunches, when they are put in the presses, since de-stalked grapes formed a solid pack, and the juice would not flow freely from the middle of the press. But the stalks formed channels between the grapes, and the juice could be expressed freely and fast, without the must taking up colour.

HOT AND COLD

The fermentation process generates heat, and it is warmth that is the main factor in colour-extraction. But heat can accelerate the fermentation process, producing wines lacking in quality. The wine-maker has to exercise judgement all the time, using every facility at his or her disposal. I remember the 1959 vintage in Beaujolais, when the weather turned very hot while the wines were being made, and many growers saw their vats producing volatile acidity. I asked one grower, whose wines were entirely free of volatile, how he had managed it. 'Each day I got up well before dawn,' he replied, 'and drove my pick up truck to the ice merchants in Lyon. I dumped the blocks of ice in the middle of the cellar, and this did the trick of keeping the whole cellar cool.'

By way of contrast, cold weather can sometimes inhibit the start of fermentation. Indeed, Fritz Hallgarten told me that one grower, unable to get a small cask of Trockenbeerenauslese to start fermenting, had put an immersion heater through the bung-hole. This was of course exceptional, since white wines especially benefit from slow cool fermentations and cooling equipment is now widely available.

Colour extraction for red wines can be achieved by leaving the skins in contact with the fermenting must for two or three weeks, but the extracted tannins may then need a longer maturing time for the wine to become smooth and drinkable. Fermenting vats are expensive to buy, take up a lot of space, and are used for only a short period of the year. So a quick, cost-effective method of colour-extractions was developed – thermo-vinification. The crushed grapes, minus the stalks, are pumped through a heat-exchanger, and flash-pasteurized momentarily, and then rapidly cooled, before being seeded with cultured yeasts to replace those killed off by the heat. The wine-making can then proceed normally. I have usually found, when tasting thermo-vinified wines, that there is a slightly 'cooked' taste. This was always the criticism, in the nineteenth century, when pasteurization was used to save wines from spoilage.

In a very hot vintage, the grapes get 'sunburnt', the skins thicken and darken, and you can get a 'roasted' taste. I think it has an extra quality of ripeness, which might distinguish it from thermo-vinification flavours. In Italy, they get some of this quality in *recioto* wines, where the individual 'sun-roasted' grapes on the shoulders *(recie)* of the bunches were originally selected for separate vinification.

Some wines nowadays are vinified by carbonic maceration, in which whole bunches are put into a closed vessel; those at the bottom are crushed by the weight of the bunches above and start fermenting, and the whole lot are bathed in warm carbon dioxide gas, helping the colour extraction. I am told that these wines have a special aroma, but so far I have been unable personally to identify it.

In many ways, this has many similarities with an old-style of vinification, when a *'pied de cuve'* of crushed grapes was created to start the fermentation, and then the whole bunches were piled up on top to fill the vat, which was then covered with a tarpaulin, and left to get on with the fermentation. But these wines were destined for long maturation, whereas the *'macération carbonique'* wines are reckoned to be quick-maturing, with relatively little staying power.

GALLO-TANNINS

Wooden casks, and especially new oak casks, can contribute to the tannin complexes of a wine. From a taster's point of view, the initial characteristics they contribute are fresh vanilla notes on the nose. But as the wine matures, the gallo-tannins seem to link with the original oeno-tannins of the wine, and produce complexes and subtleties in the nose and mouth, and a speeding-up of the early development of the wine.

Just as the '*terroir*' (soil and microclimate) of a vineyard can be perceptible in a wine, so the type and origin of the oak for the casks can now be used by the wine-maker to influence the style and flavour of his or her wines. So American oak is now distinguished from French or Scandinavian oaks, while some wine-makers may vaunt the qualities of Limousin or other regional oaks over all others.

I used to ship Cyprus Sherries to the UK in 'American barrels', which were 40-gallon casks (as compared with the 48-gallon French hogsheads). These barrels had a widely travelled career. They were originally American white oak casks for bourbon whiskey, well charred inside so that the staves could absorb fusel oils and help mature the whiskey. When they had done this job, they would be emptied, steamed out, dismantled and 'shooked': the staves were bundled together with the hoops for shipment to Italy, where they would be rebuilt in Turin to be filled with Italian Vermouth for maturing. When this was finished, they could again be steamed, shooked and shipped, this time to Cyprus, for filling with sweet Cyprus wine. There, the filled casks were left out in the open, for the wine to 'bake' in the sun, giving the mature and slightly 'maderized' style of the genre. We shipped them from Limassol to the Port of London, bottled the wine, and sold the empty casks immediately to cask merchants, who promptly sent them to Scotland for 'whisky fillings', usually some of the better grain whiskies, so that the 'sherry' flavours in the staves could colour and mature the young spirit. In a way the wheel had nearly gone full circle.

CASK SIZES

When I was training in our Bordeaux cellars, it took me quite a time to come to terms with the many sizes of casks. We bought and sold clarets by the '*tonneau*', the 900-litre casks that originated the tonnage of shipping, which was measured by the number of 'tuns' of wine a ship could carry from Bordeaux to England (or Scotland). But the notional *tonneau*, which we traded, consisted in reality of four '*barriques*' – hogsheads of 225 litres each in which the wines were matured or transported. But there were other sizes of cask around the cellar, half-hogsheads, quarters and octaves, because every time we topped up a row of casks to keep them bung-full, we were left with a partly filled cask on ullage, which needed to be transferred into smaller casks so that each would be bung-full to avoid the wine becoming oxidized.

In our Bordeaux cellars many of the less expensive wines were stored in giant casks ('*foudres*') with the contents gauged in hecto-litres. The cellar master used to talk about his younger days, when he was first mate on a tramp steamer, and had towed such large casks from Yugoslavia to France, watching them bobbing like corks on a string in the wake of his vessel.

Whenever we drew samples from a vat or a cask, we tried to draw from the middle; obviously not from the surface, which might be more oxidized, but also not from near the sides, since we believed that the wine 'breathed' through the wood. Although I no longer hold this as an article of faith, I am however persuaded that the layers of wine near the interface with the container (or indeed the air) are different from the main body of the wine. This hypothesis could explain the observed variations in behaviour between wines stored in containers of different surface-to-volume ratios. Wines in half-bottles age faster than those in bottles or magnums.

Having trained in Bordeaux, I found I had to start relearning when I went to other wine regions of France. In Burgundy, the Hogshead was a '*pièce*' and the half-cask a '*feuillette*'. In southern Burgundy (Beaujolais or Mâconnais) the standard cask was smaller – 215 litres. Did this change of surface-to-volume ratio help them to mature faster for early drinking?

9

Time and Place

WINE FASHIONS

I still remember my surprise when I was told that red wine vineyards in Bordeaux were grubbed up in the 1920s, and were replaced with white varieties. Tastes had changed, and producers were responding. When I came into the trade in 1948, people ordering a medium-dry white wine might choose an Entre-Deux-Mers, a Graves or a Hock. Dry white would be Chablis, Pouilly-Fuissé or Meursault. But Sauternes and Barsac were great favourites, possibly engendered by a craving for sweetness following wartime sugar rationing. Marketing of Yugoslav wines in the 1950s brought the name Riesling on to the public's lips. Cask shipments and UK bottlings meant that we were in a largely supply-led market.

Package holidays brought wine-drinking to a new section of the public, and containerization plus original bottlings, together with an acceptance of younger wines, permitted more demand-led marketing. Liebfraumilch vied with Yugoslav Riesling until Gresham's vinous Law came into play. Chardonnay – a name that had only rarely appeared in 'Pinot-Chardonnay-Mâcon' – became the new icon, with Cabernet Sauvignon as its red companion. The New World was becoming the new fashion in wine, and tastes conformed, meeting the current lifestyles.

Meanwhile, the Midi of France, which had traditionally furnished the 'Gros Rouge' for the 'pinard' red-wine rations for France's large armies, had to respond to the problems of Europe's 'wine lake', and replaced the high-yielding common Aramons with better varieties, tailor-made to the new tastes.

Hence the wine-taster has to adjust his or her tasting norms to changes in tastes and economics, as well as to the varying styles due to vintages and localities.

VINTAGES

The word 'vintage' in English has two meanings: the grape-harvest; and the year in which a particular wine was made. The French, however, make a distinction between the *'vendange'*, the grape-gathering, and *'millésime'*, the year of the wine. And similarly in German: *'Weinlese'* and *'Jahrgang'*.

In the nineteenth century, many wine merchants' lists offered their wines by description rather than by the year: 'best Claret' or 'Old Brown Hock'. And André L. Simon, in his Dictionary of Wine published in 1935, states:

> The chief difference between dated (Vintage) and undated (non-Vintage) wines is that the first show greater promise of improving with age and should be kept, whilst the others are ready for immediate consumption and may – but need not – be kept.

The prevalence of vintage indications has developed mightily in the last half-century, so that everyday wines, which in past eras would have been non-Vintage, now show their year of origin. They may even carry the equivalent of a 'best before . . .' recommendation. But such wines also reflect the vast improvement in wine-making skills, since they seem to be of largely similar quality year on year. It is in the higher echelons of the wine world that weather variations from vintage to vintage can be more clearly distinguished.

The logic behind vintage variations should be sought in the fact that Western Europe (and its classic wine-lands) may be influenced by the weather patterns coming from the west, with the approach of Atlantic highs and lows, and changes in the moderating effects of the Gulf Stream. Mediterranean vineyards are less affected, and Burgundy is partly shielded from the west by the Massif Central of France, and Burgundian weather patterns seem to be largely governed by northerly or southerly winds.

It has been averred that New World wines are less prone to vintage variations, but this may not be strictly true of all of them.

It might apply to Argentinian wines, but if we look at the wines of Chile we may find their climate and weather patterns different from what might be expected. Although the Andes run north and south, many of the good vineyards lie in east–west valleys, such as Maipo. You would expect cooler conditions nearer to the South Pole, and greater heat nearer the equator. But you would then be ignoring the effects of the cold Humboldt current, flowing northwards along the Chilean coast, and cooling some of the more northerly vineyard areas. Again, you would have to watch out for the influence of 'El Niño' (and its secondary effect 'La Niña') upsetting the prevalent patterns of currents and wind-flows in the Pacific Basin; these may also affect the Californian coastline.

PROPINQUITY

While I was training in Bordeaux, I seemed to meet a number of Graves wines with a faintly resinous quality. When I remarked on it, I was reminded that parts of the Graves district were quite close to plantations of turpentine pines (prevalent in the Landes), so it was reasonable to expect that grapes might pick up a whiff of the resin when the trees were being tapped. But I do not seem to have met it for quite a long time, so I begin to wonder whether it was my imagination, or whether I might now be less sensitive to it, or whether the trees have been cut down or burnt by forest fires.

I am still not being allowed to forget the time when I was lecturing to a group of Master of Wine students, and I had suggested that one might be able to identify a certain vintage of Pommard, because the roads in the commune had been sprayed with tar that summer, and that a whiff of tar in the Pommard wine might give a clear marker. At the time I thought it was a helpful suggestion. After all, in those bad old days there were quite a lot of wines from outside the *appellation* masquerading as Pommard, in spite of all the regulations and controls.

WINE GUMS

Holidaymakers in Greece may have undergone bad experiences in tavernas due to poor-quality retsinas, and wondered why people should have bothered to put resin into wine. In the past, when asked this question, I sometimes answered frivolously that in ancient times wine-makers had made their wines in heavy amphoras, and then transported them in lighter goatskins, following up with the question 'How do you wine-proof a goatskin?', and then suggesting that you might tan it inside with resins; hence raising the question: which taste would be preferable – resin or goat?

It would however have been more helpful to have asked how, in a hot climate, can you keep a table wine in drinkable condition through the summer? Ribéreau-Gayon's text-book on wine-making suggests the possible presence in wines of 'protective colloids', and delves into the use of gum arabic as a stabilizing agent in wines. Dr John Storer of Glasgow, writing in the *Encyclopaedia Britannica* (ninth edition 1880), told us that the purest gum arabic was Turkey Picked, and suggested that it might be a form of unfermentable glucoside. Retsina uses locally available Greek resin, but unfortunately many of the base wines have in the past been of lowish quality. Do not let this put you off; good-quality retsinas are being made by some of the leading producers, including Cambas's excellent rosé retsina, made from the pink-skinned Moschofilero grape, and it marries very happily with hors-d'oeuvres and mezes.

Dry vermouth is another wine that unexpectedly goes well with salty and spicy starter dishes. Many of the vermouth ingredients have febrifuge and restorative attributes, making me wonder whether malarial symptoms from the Pontine Marshes may have contributed to the favour of Italian vermouth (long before the cocktail era), and similarly for French vermouth with the low-lying lands of the Rhône estuary. The principal ingredient of French vermouth is the eponymous wormwood (the time-honoured vermifuge) from which it derived its name, whereas Italian Vermouth relies on Roman Wormwood as its main ingredient. Many of the other traditional vermouth ingredients will be found playing a role in alternative medicine.

10

Climate and Ambience

═══════

WINE-SHIPPING CHOICES

In bygone days, most wine was produced for local consumption, and it was the exceptional wines that found favour outside the region, and were exported. Even then, logistics counted, and chance came into play. The building of a canal allowed the wines of Monbazillac to be shipped to the Netherlands, where they became popular. It was the exceptional height of a South Burgundy wine-grower that attracted the king's attention in church, and led to his wines being introduced to the court.

Modern marketing now allows a far wider choice for distribution, but there still remain many limiting factors: the time-scales needed for planting vines and producing grapes are still very long; and even the most skilled marketers cannot always make the consumer swallow the spiel and enjoy the product.

So the wine merchant still needs to study and understand the many variations in lifestyle and taste across the clientele, and make allowances for the effect of climate on appreciation. Holiday moods allow us to enjoy food and wine differently from our everyday habits, and even hardened wine-buyers are not immune to the charms of the wine-producing areas. So they have to practise restraint and judgement. Typically, they must say to themselves: 'This wine is delicious here, but how will it taste on a rainy Sunday in Manchester?' They have to think in parallel, balancing the emotional and the practical.

11

Wine Practicalities

FINING OR FILTERING

When I was doing my early training in cellar-work, it was accepted that we either fined or filtered the wine before bottling (and occasionally both). I had in mind a picture: that particles were floating in the wine, which we had to remove. So we either passed the wine through a net (i.e. the filter mesh), or else created a mesh (the finings) which slowly sank down, taking the particles with it. The better wines were fined, while the more ordinary qualities were filtered; it was a quicker and more cost-effective process.

I now find that, although I still keep this simple view before me, I also have to accept that 'adsorption' is occurring, and that this might be envisaged either in molecular or in electromagnetic terms. I now also imagine sponge-like structures, which either suck the particles into their pores or hold them there by electromagnetic attraction. When we had very young wines coming into our Bordeaux cellars, and we had to process considerable volumes of white wines in rapid succession, we used to pump them through cloth filters; the interstices of the cloth had to be endued with infusorial or diatomaceous earth; this was stirred into a quantity of the wine, which was then pumped round and round through the filter, until the 'filter aid' had built up in layers on the filter cloth or filter pads, and the wine was coming through 'star-bright'. We could then pump the mass of the wine through the filter and clarify it. The filter aid was made up of the countless skeletons of microscopic infusoria or diatoms, some of which, when viewed under a powerful microscope, looked rather like snowflakes, and doubtless adsorbed the wine's impurities within their angular structures.

When we shipped wines in cask for bottling in our London cellars, we occasionally needed to fine them, to ensure their stability in bottle. I remember there were two hogsheads of white Graves Supérieures which needed to be gelatine-fined. I weighed out the required amount of high-quality powdered gelatine, dissolved it in warm water, let it cool, whisked it up in some of the wine, and divided it into two equal portions. I decided to fine one cask, while the head cellarman would fine the other one. We each poured our finings through the bung-hole of our cask, and then proceeded to 'rouse' the cask. We each took a clean broom-handle, put it into the wine through the bung-hole, and stirred the wine vigorously with it. The object was to disperse the finings equally into every part of the cask. We roused the wine in each cask for the same length of time, but I was envious of Fred Kettle's flick of the wrist, which seemed to send the finings into the furthermost corners of his cask. Needless to say, his cask fell bright five days before mine. Which goes to show that knowledge is not the same as know-how.

In those days, most finings were carried out according to rule-of-thumb formulae. For fine red wines, white of egg (albumen) was used, and isinglass was the preferred fining for top-quality white wines. Gelatine was the standby for the more ordinary wines, both white and red. I have an idea that the pH of a wine may also influence the choice, whether to use isinglass or gelatine. These finings would be introduced into the wine in colloidal form, and would interact with tannins and/or colloids in the wine to create flocculation. The rate of sedimentation of these flakes into the lees at the bottom of the cask, and the degree of adsorption of impurities by the flakes, would determine the effectiveness of the fining.

As soon as finings have settled into the lees, it is customary to 'rack' the casks, i.e., to draw off the clear wine into a fresh cask, leaving the deposits behind. Cask wines need to be racked at regular intervals, since there could be a risk of a wine becoming contaminated with a 'lees taste' or smell, if dead yeasts remain too long in a cask. There are, however, exceptions to this: sherries, and '*élevage sur lie*', especially for Muscadet.

Fine white burgundies are occasionally matured with *élevage sur lie*, and the late Monsieur Henri Gouges used an interesting variant of it, for his white Nuits-St-Georges 'Les Perrières'. After the first racking to get rid of the heavy lees from the yeast fermentation, the wine still contained some lighter floating lees, which seem to be necessary to activate the malolactic fermentation lactobacilli. He then added a mineral fining – bentonite (named after Fort Benton in the USA) – to each cask. Bentonite has adsorptive powers, so the light lees agglomerated to the bentonite, and settled to the bottom. Any trace off-flavours from the lees would then be adsorbed by the bentonite, thus preventing taints from occurring. At regular intervals, the casks were 'roused', dispersing the bentonite and its attendant ferments throughout the wine. This had a number of effects: a slow but steady malolactic fermentation was maintained, for as long as eighteen months, with carbon dioxide gas becoming dissolved in the wine, inhibiting oxidation, and maintaining a reductive situation. Dispersing the yeast traces through the wine had a bleaching effect, keeping his wine water-white in colour and fresh-flavoured, while elements from the yeasts added to the body and richness of the wine. It was particularly significant in the case of this particular wine, because the vineyard was planted not with the customary Chardonnay but with Pinot Blanc, which can have a tendency to broaden in flavour and oxidize faster than Chardonnay.

There seem to be so many variables at work when a wine is being fined that scientific considerations become complicated – hence the rule-of-thumb approach. We were always taught the importance of 'rousing the wine' thoroughly, sufficiently to introduce bubbles of air into the wine – which seemed odd when we had previously been trying so hard to prevent excessive oxidation with sulphur and topping-up. But it makes sense when you learn that traces of iron are linked to the tannins in a wine, and the ferrous or ferric state of the iron affects the 'take' of the finings. Introducing oxygen into the wine, by stirring in air, can change the iron from bivalent form to trivalent, helping it to link with the fining agent.

THE ISOELECTRIC POINT OF TANNIN

These electromagnetic effects seem to come into play when wines are maturing, and may even be brought to bear during wine-tasting. So we should try to devote some effort to understanding the general patterns that seem to be involved.

Wines start their lives with a relatively high acidity, which may reduce during maturation through three main effects: reduction in the 'green-apple' malic acid, generally through a malolactic fermentation; reduction in the 'wine acid' tartaric, usually through crystallization and dropping-out into the lees; and esterification, the development of aromas by the linking of acids and alcohols.

The tannins in a wine carry an electrical charge, and when the acidity of the wine drops to a certain point, known as the 'isoelectric point of tannin', the tannins in the wine flip their charge (say, from positive to negative, or maybe vice versa), become attracted to substances in the wine which they had previously repelled, and link up with them. This seems (at least in part) to be the mechanism actuating the flocculation of a fining, and it explains how a wine in cask can (quite suddenly) throw out a lot of colouring materials into the lees. The same sort of thing can also happen in bottle, when a wine 'throws a crust'.

CHEWING THE TANNINS

When we spit out a red wine, the tannins have coagulated. Our alkaline saliva has neutralized the acidity of the wine, and the tannins have passed their isoelectric point. Maybe we could use this occurrence to help us in our tasting skills.

When the wine is in the glass, the tannins are in solution. When it comes into the mouth, changes are going to occur. Earlier on, we had floated the idea that we might be able to assess the time that our saliva needed to cancel the wine's acidity; now we need to relate the time-sequence idea to the behaviour of the tannins in the mouth.

'Chew' the wine until the saliva is well mixed in, then press the tongue against the hard palate. You may well sense a 'grittiness' from the particles of coagulated tannins. Spit it out, take a fresh sample of wine into the mouth, run it into each cheek, put your tongue in your cheek, and see if you can sense a certain 'furriness' inside the cheeks. Check the colour of the wine against the two mouth-feel sensations, and see whether you can establish any relationship, or difference gradient, and whether either of them might relate to the colour intensity of the wine. Finally, chew a fresh sample of wine, and see if there is a time-lapse before you first feel the grittiness against the palate.

There is not a great chance of finding a directly linear relationship, since judging the quantity of tannins (difficult enough to analyse in the old days) may now be obfuscated by the qualitative idea of 'ripe' or 'unripe' tannins (or the current differentiation between 'hard' or 'soft' tannins), and the different styles of wood-notes; apart from the various types of oak, you also have the variants of cask-fermentation, and/or cask-maturation, wood-chips or wood-powders. The object of training exercises such as these is not necessarily to obtain clever answers, but to concentrate the mind, and intensify the acuities.

The other important reason for 'chewing' your wine sample is to discover flavour- and aroma-factors, which may be masked by predominant tannins. By mixing the wine with your saliva you have taken the tannins past their isoelectric point, and by coagulating them you have taken them out of solution and into suspension. And by drawing air into the mouth, and bubbling it through the wine, you may be able to glean an inkling of how the wine will present itself in a year or two's time, when the tannins may be less assertive.

I learnt a lesson about unripe tannins when I was training in our Bordeaux cellars, in 1948. We had quite a large stock of a 1937 St Emilion, a lesser château red wine, which was not evolving at all, because its hard tannins were inhibiting the maturing process, and making it virtually undrinkable. Maybe this was why it had survived, and not been commandeered by the Germans during the 1939–45 war! So we were given the task of disgorging it, uncorking each bottle and tipping the contents back into casks. We then fined the wine fairly severely with gelatine, and when the finings had settled out into the bottom of the casks, we bottled it off again through a filter. It had lost a lot of colour, and emerged as a very ordinary wine, but at least it was drinkable; the oxygenation had made it look and taste its age, and we had a saleable product for less choosy restaurants who were keen to have some older vintages on their lists.

THE SWEETNESS OF OLD RED WINE

One of the special delights of a fully mature old red wine is the lingering sweetness that so flatters the palate. We were always told in the old days that this was 'fruit' that had previously been masked by the tannins, and that only when the tannins had thrown out into sediment and crust in the bottle, and the wine had been religiously decanted, could it emerge and show its character. As this seemed to be an article of faith with many respected pundits, for quite a long time I accepted this. But as I became more adept at 'chewing the tannins' (see above), I became persuaded that the 'fruit' that emerged from under such tannins bore no relationship to the flavours that I was finding in the old wines. And I could not envisage how the one could transmogrify into the other.

When I discussed this with Jules Chauvet, he suggested that this might only be occurring in wines that had thrown a sediment, and he put forward the hypothesis that what we were observing was the result of a breakdown or autolysis of anthocyanins, or of complexes of polypeptides or proteins with tannins that had been deposited over the years in the bottle. He suggested that each time an anthocyanin broke down in this manner a glycoside might emerge, and that when enough of such glycosides had been created they could register on the palate as the observed lingering sweetness of a fine old wine. I can only hope that if this should prove to be true, the present tendency of technically brilliant wine-makers producing wines that seldom if ever produce a sediment will not result in the eventual total disappearance of this wonderful taste-sensation.

12

Multiple Balancing

FOUR-WAY ASSESSMENT

We have already seen some of the problems of balance, for the wine-maker, between alcohol, acidity and sugars in white wines, or alcohol, acidity and tannins in dry red wines, and the wine-taster's eventual reaction to them. When tasting port, and particularly vintage ports, you need to bring yet another balance factor into consideration, since you are tasting and evaluating a red wine (with alcohol, acids and tannins), but also with residual sugars, giving sweetness and richness.

For the wine-maker, it is a challenge to achieve the perfect equilibrium between acidity, sweetness, tannins and alcohol. It must be an imaginative and creative process, thinking ahead to the time when the wine will be maturing in bottle, how each of these elements may evolve and interact, and planning for the time when the wine-lover will wish to enjoy it.

It starts, of course, in the vineyard, watching the ripening of the grapes, the rise in sugar levels, the drop in acidity, and the ripening of the tannins with the colour and thickness of the skins. Changes in the weather may influence the timing of the grape harvest; then, when the grapes are crushed and starting to ferment, ambient temperatures may influence the rate of change of the sugars into alcohol, and the degree and intensity of colour extraction.

Of course, if the wine-maker is aiming to make a fine dry tawny port – which can be a splendid aperitif wine – he will let it fully ferment until all the sugars have turned into alcohol, add a modicum of grape spirit to bring it up to full strength, and then age it for a number of years in cask, so that much of the red colour falls out into the lees, and the remainder can oxidize to the tawny colour of a lion's mane, with the alcohol, acids and flavour tannins maturing together to produce a nutty taste.

But for vintage port, he needs to let it ferment only long enough to reach the desired colour extraction, and for fermentation aromas to develop which may eventually meld with the vinosity of the alcohol; most of all, he needs to retain sufficient residual sugars to give richness and succulence to balance the warmth and attack of the grape brandy that he will now add, to stop the fermentation, and bring the wine up to the desired strength of 21 degrees of alcohol by volume.

Changes will occur in the wine during its two years in cask, before it is bottled as vintage port. The addition of alcohol to stop the fermentation will have affected the solubility of the tartaric acid content of the wine, causing part of it to fall out into the lees as potassium bitartrate (see Table 2). This in turn will alter the acidity (pH) of the young wine, and may trigger a fall-out of some

Table 2
Solubility of potassium bitartrate (potassium hydrogen tartrate) in water and alcohol

Temperature (°c)	Solubility (in grams per litre) in water containing the stated percentages of alcohol			
	0%	10%	20%	30%
0	0.30	0.17	0.11	0.07
5	0.32	0.19	0.13	0.07
10	0.41	0.21	0.16	0.09
15	0.44	0.24	0.16	0.09
20	0.49	0.29	0.17	0.11
25	0.54	0.36	0.21	0.12
30	0.69	0.40	0.25	0.13
35	0.84	0.49	0.29	0.19
40	0.96	0.54	0.38	0.23
45	1.13	0.73	0.44	0.26
50	1.25	0.87	0.54	0.30

of the tannins. So the balancing act goes on, aided by judicious rackings and finings, until the wine is stable and fit to bottle. The process does not end there; bottle-ageing starts, crusts and sediments may be deposited, while a slow oxidation takes place. This does not depend solely on the small amounts of air that may reach the wine through the cork; auto-oxidation can take place as a result of chemical changes in the wine.

The wine-tasters must realize that they are meeting the wine somewhere along this time-continuum; they must try to find out where they are, either actually, or relatively. (The usual way is to ask someone who knows more than you do!) Now can come the work of constructive imagination: working backwards to try to judge what the wine-makers were trying to do, and how successful they may have been; and then to try to project forwards.

One way to start is to listen to pundits when they say that a certain new wine reminds them of a previous vintage; if you can get an opportunity to taste this previous vintage in its current state, and compare and contrast it with the new wine, you may be able to establish two points along the evolutionary continuum of the older wine (one real, from your tasting of the wine as it is now, and the other earlier point, by analogy, from your notes on the new young vintage). You should then, in your mind, create two similar points along the continuum of the new vintage (one real, from your earlier tasting of the new wine, the other by analogy from your tasting of the older vintage: see page 64). You can think of it being like the playing of two different notes on the lower register of a piano, and then copying them an octave or two higher.

The other, slower way of achieving forward projection is to taste the same wine over a period of years, and to record the changes. This gives you a series of points along the life-cycle of a style of wine, and whenever you come across similarities in another wine, you may be able to compare and contrast, backwards and forwards, imagining the origins of the new wine, and prognosticating its future.

13
Wine Patterns

DUNNE'S THEORY OF TIME

In the late 1920s, J. W. Dunne's widely discussed book, *An Experiment with Time*, put forward the idea that the arrow of time might not always go forwards in a straight line, but that one should be willing to consider the concepts of circular time, or parallel time. The author J. B. Priestley took up the ideas, and wrote a series of highly successful 'time plays', some of which are still being performed.

Around the same period, the philosopher G. I. Gurdjieff was teaching the mental exercise of 'thinking in canon'. This was by analogy to the musical pattern of a 'canon', whereby a melody starts, and (after a few notes) another voice or instrument starts the same tune, so that the two (or more) blend and harmonize. Simple examples of the canon are 'London's Burning', 'Frère Jacques', and 'Three Blind Mice' (see Figures 4 and 5).

Quite apart from the difficulty of accepting and executing such mental acrobatics, the wine-taster is faced with the problem of recording, and recalling evanescent percepts. Some are relatively easy: you can parallel the colour continuum of a red wine, from its initial purple-red, through to a final brick-red or orange-brown of an onion-skin, against a longer or shorter time-scale. Others are much harder to quantify.

MORE GESTALT PSYCHOLOGY

Although I have always recorded tasting notes in a normal manner, and continue to do so, I have for many years reinforced them with

Figure 4
Tasting in canon

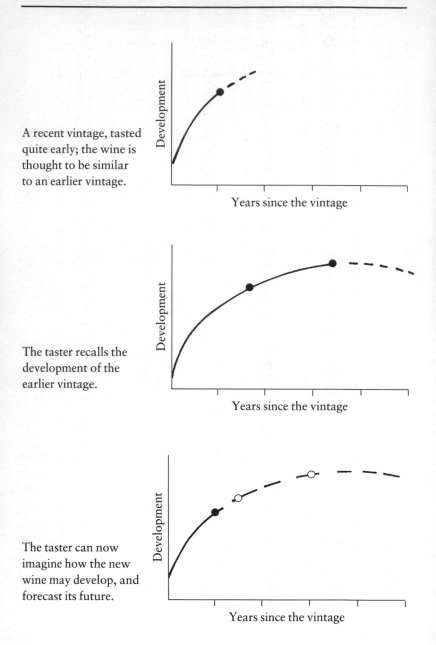

A recent vintage, tasted quite early; the wine is thought to be similar to an earlier vintage.

Development

Years since the vintage

The taster recalls the development of the earlier vintage.

Development

Years since the vintage

The taster can now imagine how the new wine may develop, and forecast its future.

Development

Years since the vintage

Figure 5
'London's burning'

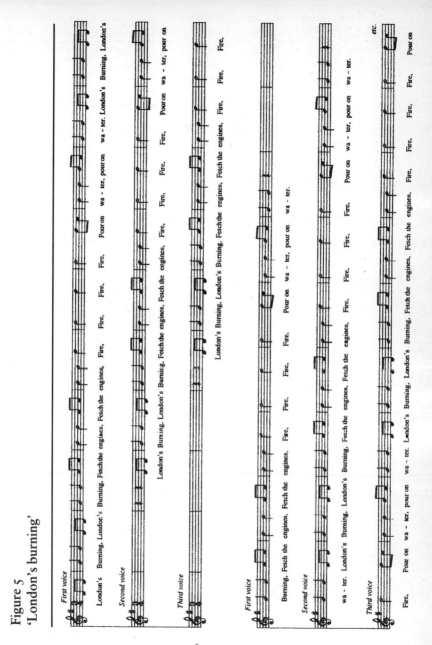

a mental 'image' of the wine. This started quite early on in my tasting career, when (for example) I had tasted a wide range of St Emilion wines, and certain common factors seemed to emerge, so that I started to formulate a 'shape' of St Emilion wine, as against Médoc or Graves.

Years earlier, in an encyclopaedia, I had seen an article on ethnic types, and it had been illustrated by a photographic trick: over-laying a series of negatives of (say) North American Indians, or Pacific Melanesians, and printing the result; producing a blurred but recognizable image accentuating the salient characteristics. In like manner, I found that my mind was creating a series of 'photofit images' of St Emilion wines on transparent sheets, which, when laid one over the other, gave me the generic image.

Over the years, I had opportunities of tasting the same vintage wine at intervals, and I seemed to make a 'photofit image' of the wine at each stage of its development; hence I found I could re-create mental images of the wine's shape changing as it matured. As a child I had played with little paper booklets on which cartoon characters were drawn on successive pages with slight changes in their attitudes; if you flipped through them fast, the figures appeared to move. In my mind, I played a similar game with the maturing wines, comparing and contrasting the rates at which the developing shapes altered.

WINE SHAPES

My interest in this subject received a boost when I was told that some people never bothered to use words when taking notes at a wine-tasting, but simply scribbled down an image. I had just been asked to give a talk on wine-tasting to the Society of Hedonists of Sir John Cass College, in London, and I took the opportunity to ask if I could conduct a tasting experiment, and asked them to provide a couple of statisticians to assess the result.

I selected for the tasting a light Moselle, a medium-dry Graves, a rich Sauternes, a red Bordeaux, a red burgundy, and a Château-neuf-du-Pape. Against each wine was a series of shapes, with a space for them to draw in their own shape, if they so desired. Each of the participants was asked to taste each wine, mark which shape

Figure 6
Wine-shapes tasting form

Moselle

Sauternes

Médoc

Château neuf-
du-Pape

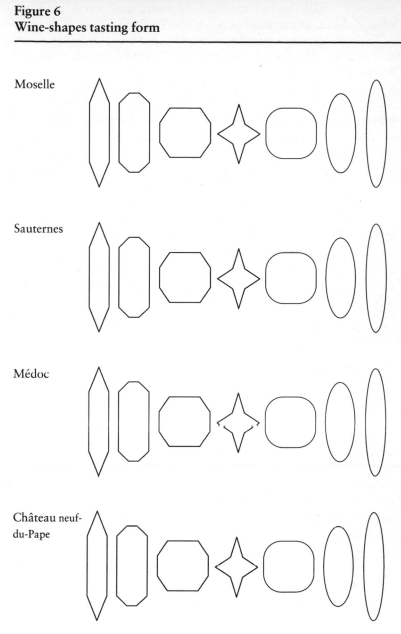

approximated to their impression of the wine, or to draw their own idea (see Figure 6).

The tasting sheets were then collected for analysis by the statisticians, who, after a cursory examination, stated that there seemed to be some statistical significance, so they took them away for more detailed study. The added shapes drawn by some of the participants were rather weird, recalling Rorschach blots, and seemed to relate more to the taster's psyche than to the wines.

In due course, I was sent a statistical report, which seemed to show a correlation between the type of wine and wine shapes, and it was published with my report of the experiment, in *Harpers Wine and Spirit Gazette*. A lively correspondence then ensued in *Harpers*, during which my leg was unmercifully pulled. The editor kindly allowed me to close the correspondence, by publishing a letter in which I explained that the Hedonists' tasting was intended as the first of a series, culminating in a three-dimensional blind tasting, in which the participants would be physically blindfolded. They would be required to select from a series of boxes a three-dimensional object corresponding to the shape of the wine; ranging from (for example) a plastic porcupine to a 'super-egg'. But, I warned, the difficulty in organizing such a tasting was that if there were too many 'round' wines, the answers would be a lot of balls.

FORWARD PROJECTIONS

A wine-taster needs a good memory. A good filing system for tasting-notes will help, but cannot play the same role. Tasting-notes can help to recall forgotten details, and trigger memory. One also needs plenty of tasting experience over a period of time in order to gauge effectively the future of a wine.

First, you have to recall a wine, tasted in the past, with similar characteristics; you then try to remember how this earlier wine has turned out. But as you seldom have a 100 per cent perfect match, you then have to compare and contrast the current wine with the earlier one, in order to pinpoint the similarities and differences. If you are following the 'photofit' parallel, the similarities will give you a straightforward projection to the future, while differences will change or distort the images ahead.

This first comparison will give you an approximation of the time required for the new wine to develop. The greater the differences in detail with the earlier wine, the larger will be the margins of error in the time-scale of your projections. To reduce vagueness, and achieve a degree of precision, more work is required. Each of the following operations interact, and you need constantly to check their influence and weighting.

Each vintage is the result of different weather patterns, favourable weather yielding a better vintage; in general terms, the better vintages last longer. But the weather patterns may favour one variety of grape more than another. This can be particularly significant in Bordeaux, where three main grapes – Cabernet Sauvignon, Cabernet Franc, and Merlot – can ripen at different rates. As a rough guide, in the fine vineyards of the Médoc, Cabernet Sauvignon is king, whereas across the river the Merlot may predominate. Merlot can ripen earlier, while Cabernet Sauvignon takes longer, and tends to give longer-lasting wines. So watch out for 'Merlot years' or 'Cabernet years'. The proportion of the different varieties (*encépagement*) in an estate tends to be fairly static, since replanting is expensive, and needs to be a long-term investment. But if the estate has changed hands, and a replanting has occurred in the interim between your two samples, it might falsify your deductions. There may also be overall changes in planting patterns, such as more Merlot being planted in place of grubbed-up Cabernet Sauvignon, because Merlot is more reliable in the less good years.

Again, if the estate has changed hands, or a new wine-maker has been appointed, you may need to allow for different wine-making techniques. The colour of a red wine, and the quality of the tannins may give clues to the length of time the grape-skins have been macerated in the must, while vanilla notes on the nose may indicate a higher proportion of new wood in the vinification or maturing. Grape tannins can influence longevity, while new-oak tannins can produce earlier complexing of aromas.

Light fruity wines are generally quicker-maturing, while those where the fruit-notes seem masked by tannins and acidity can appear 'steely' or severe, and likely to need more time.

ESTIMATING LONGEVITY

Time and again, when making my tasting-notes, I find myself noting a wine as a 'keeper', and another one as 'quick-maturing', or even 'forward'. I may even put down a spread of dates, from the time I reckon it will show its real quality, to the time when I guess it may cease to improve (e.g. 1999–2011).

With dry red wines, I am probably carrying out a three-way assessment, evaluating alcohol, acidity and tannins. French tasters have evolved a triangular diagram to illustrate the concept (see p. 38). But in reality, a skilled taster may bring further factors into the equation. Before taking the wine into the mouth, the nose may have identified varietal notes, or even soil and subsoil character-istics.

When I used to lecture on wines, I promulgated the 'Artillery-man's Guide to Burgundy'. I explained that for long-range you used a field-gun; to shoot over hills and for medium-range, a howitzer was used; and for short-range, a mortar (Figure 7a). This was paralleled with an illustrative graph indicating that top Côte de Nuits red wines could be longest-lasting, Côte de Beaune somewhat quicker-maturing, while single-vineyard crus of Beaujolais (such as Morgon, Côte de Brouilly, and Moulin-à-Vent) could be excellent, though relatively short-lived (Figure 7b). This could be explained by a difference of '*terroir*' between Côte de Nuits and Côte de Beaune wines, and a difference of '*cépage*' (grape variety) between the Côte-d'Or (Pinot Noir) and South Burgundy (Gamay).

If you wish, you can develop the 'variety and *terroir*' concept with a compare-and-contrast tasting of Beaujolais and Mâconnais wines, both made from Gamay grapes, but with different soil types. The archetypal Beaujolais subsoil is granitic, giving lightish, but brilliant, colour, with flower-notes on the nose, and refreshing fruity flavours. The Mâconnais soils are generally calcareous (chalky or limy), which tends to produce red wines with deeper colour, darker tones, and more leathery notes on the nose than in wines made from the Gamay grape. You can also get Pinot Noir wines in the Mâconnais, as well as 'Passe-tout-grains' made from a Gamay/Pinot Noir mixture.

Figure 7a
The Artilleryman's Guide to Burgundy

Field Gun – shooting straight and far

Howitzer – shooting over obstacles

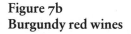

Mortar – shorter-range shooting

Figure 7b
Burgundy red wines

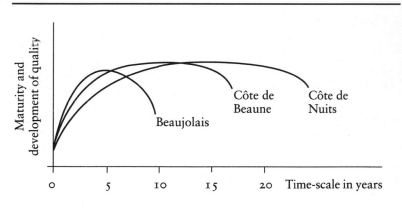

14

Finding Your Place

═══════════

MORE ABOUT *TERROIR*

If you ever get the chance to learn about a wine district in detail, you start to discover delightful anomalies: the difference between Brouilly and Côte de Brouilly becomes clear when you see that the sugar-loaf shape of the Côte de Brouilly is due to a porphyry extrusion through the generality of granite. In Moulin-à-Vent there is a '*lieu-dit*', or '*finage*' (as individual site-names are known locally) called Les Brasses, where the silica-sand soil type gives the young wine in casks an appetizing smell of newly baked crusty bread! As the wine matures, this changes into an aroma of roasted almonds.

It was this kind of specialized and detailed knowledge that enabled an amateur wine-taster – an electrical engineer by profession – to become the greatest authority on the wines of Barbaresco (in Piedmont, Northern Italy), able to identify individual vineyard sites, their growers, and the vintages, in a blind tasting. But then he had spent every holiday in the district, assiduously visiting the growers, discussing and assessing, and learning in detail how it had been done.

I often use the term 'steely' to describe the white burgundy from the Mâconnais parish of Viré, to distinguish it from other wines of the region, and in particular from the wines of the nearby parish of Clessé, which often have a milder and spicier aroma, due to a particular clone, known locally as 'Chardonnay Musqué'. There is now a new *appellation*, covering both districts, and named Viré-Clessé.

In the past, I had used the characteristics of another Chardonnay clone as a useful identifier. It gave a roast-chestnut aroma and flavour to the wine, and I had found it particularly in the wines of Corton-Charlemagne. But I have since come across it in Californian Chardonnay wines, so I must now assume that it is one of the recommended 'Davis clones' promoted by the University of California-Davis wine department.

Julian Jeffs uses a 'buttery' flavour (see p. 93) to identify some of the Chardonnays grown in the Meursault district.

SOILS AND SUBSOILS

Although there are several rootstocks in use which are shallow-rooting and spreading (useful when the water table is high), I think you will find that most grapevine varieties prefer to be deep-rooting. The ancient world made use of this, and its vestiges may still be seen in parts of Tuscany, in Italy. Despite the modern preference for monoculture, you may yet find traces of classic polyculture, with widely spaced rows of olive trees separated by wheat-sown plough-land, and grapevines growing up the olive trees, and trained along ropes looped from tree to tree with their leaf canopy and grape bunches hanging in swags.

The olive tree has two different kinds of roots: fibrous roots for about a metre round the trunk for nutrition, and water-seeking roots, sometimes as thick as a man's arm, extending up to twenty metres. (A gardener's parallel to this would be ring-culture of tomatoes.) These water-seeking roots would stretch out under the wheatland, and would not compete excessively with the cereal crop, which would be ripening for harvesting in July, whereas olives are gathered towards November. But the olive's fibrous roots would oblige the vine to root into the cool subsoil, reducing yields, but intensifying the soil characteristics of the eventual wine, to be harvested around September. So the land produced the classic nourishment of bread, oil and wine.

When I was training in Bordeaux, I kept trying to find explanations for the difference in style between the various Médoc districts; the subsoils seemed to hint at a pattern (see Table 3). I now suspect that it may have been an oversimplification. Nevertheless, I kept coming back to the influence of subsoil, especially when Dr Renato Ratti taught me about the Barolo soils and subsoils, and

Table 3
Soils and sub-soils of red Bordeaux districts

District	Soil	Sub-soil	Comments
Margaux	Sand and gravel	Gravel and ferruginous	Pure-flavoured classic claret, owing its character in part to the soil – with gravel bringing out Cabernet style, and the iron content giving tannin and long-lasting characteristics.
St Julien	Fertile gravel	Alios[1]; marne[2] (marl) in a few places	Fuller, rounder and fruitier style; there is a clear style – difference between Beychevelle-St Julien and the rest of the commune.
Pauillac	Heavy gravel	Deep alios	Pauillac produces a number of the finest clarets; the gravel can develop the Cabernet style, and the deep alios the velvety depth of flavour.
St Estèphe	Fertile gravel	Fairly deep alios in some places (particularly to north). Elsewhere stony clay.	Some similarity to Pauillac, but with less depth of flavour and more firmness; this is partly due to some calcareous soil in the westerly part of the commune.
St Emilion			
(a) Hills	Chalky-clay or ferruginous	Stone or rock	The rocky hills of St Emilion have high mineralization giving lasting qualities (e.g. Ch. Ausone), with some parallels to Margaux, but with more fatness and roundness due to the different proportions of grape varieties.
(b) Plain	Sand or sandy gravel	Gravel and ferruginous alios	The gravel plain that extends into Pomerol is equivalent to the lower terraces of the Haut Médoc, and the depth of gravel can produce full deep-styled wine like Ch. Cheval Blanc.
Pomerol			
(a) East	Sandy gravel	Gravel	Gravel as in St Emilion plain produces character and finesse in Ch. Pétrus, equalling Ch. Lafite in value.
(b) West	Sandy	Iron-pan	Produces wine with less body, equivalent to bourgeois growth Haut Médoc clarets.

NOTE 1 Subsoils of alios (a kind of coarse brown sandstone) are impervious to water (like clay). If level, they tend to make the soil damp; if sloping, they can make the soil too dry, as water runs down them. Deep digging makes them suitable for vines.

NOTE 2 Subsoils of marne (marl) are hard and semi-pervious to water. For vineyards they are broken up with pickaxes and mixed with the topsoil. More suitable for white grapes.

District	Soil	Sub-soil	Comments
Côtes de Canon-Fronsac			
(a) Tertre de Fronsac	Calcareous clays	Quarry-stone	The steep-sided stony hill of the Tertre produces firm, slow-maturing wines; the lime produces longevity in the red wine, and the steely style comes from the stone.
(b) Coteaux	Clayey gravels	Stony	Similar style, but less accentuated.
Côtes de Fronsac			
(a) Côtes	Calcareous clays, including fossil limestone	Stony, with clay in places	Similar styles to the above, but less quality and repute.
(b) Sables	Alluvium	Sand or gravel	Lighter, supple wines, quicker-maturing.
(c) Palus	Rich alluvium	Clay	Fuller, rounder, rich-coloured, useful commercial wines.
St. André-de-Cubzac	Sandy clay, some chalky clay;	Stony to north and north west; clay elsewhere.	The Cubzaguais zone, together with the Bourgeais and the western part of the Blayais, form a geological unity with part of the Entre-Deux-Mers and the Premières Côtes de Bordeaux. But the Cubzac zone only has rights to the *Appellations* 'Bordeaux' and 'Bordeaux Supérieur'.
Côtes de Bourg	Chalky clay	Stone or freestone	The Bourgeais region produces well-rounded wines with some similarities to St. Emilion, but less quality.
Côtes de Blaye and Premières Côtes de Blaye	Sandy clay or chalky clay; pure sand at extreme east	Limestone in west; iron-pan towards east. Extreme east, clay or stone.	The western part of the Blayais has similarities to the Bourgeais, but some of the wines tend to be coarse and more tannic. The eastern part of the Blayais has geological affinities to the neighbouring Cognac zones.

related them to the kind of wines made in that Piedmont area (see Figure 8 and Table 4). One of the characteristics of the Nebbiolo grape (used to produce Barolo) is that on certain soil it can produce a particular tarry (*catrame*) style. Geologically, the soils of Barolo can be found stratified horizontally, dissected by rivers, and although the strata may originally have been distinctive, and striping the hillsides horizontally, erosion has often mixed them together; this combined soil often produces the best Barolos, combining the elegance of the lighter soils with the long-lasting depth from the stronger soils.

When I had a house in the Languedoc region of the south of France, the nearby vineyard area of the Costières du Gard was applying to be upgraded from *vin de qualité supérieur* (VdQS) to *appellation contrôlée* (AC), and their submissions gave details of the soils and subsoils; and I was struck by the parallels with the Barolo soils. The region now has the *appellation contrôlée* Costières de Nîmes. They do not make similar wines for two reasons: different grapes, and the reflected ultraviolet light from the Alps in May on to the Barolo vines.

IN PRAISE OF OLDER VINES

Some growers make a special *cuvée* of their oldest vines, label the bottles '*vieilles vignes*', and usually charge extra for the enhanced quality that the old vines are deemed to bring. This opinion is hallowed by time, and would seem to be based on three main factors. Root development has generally continued, despite yearly pruning of the canopy; hence the roots-to-branches ratio has increased, and the extract of soil minerals should have intensified. Secondly, the vine-stock has grown in girth, providing reserves for grape production. Thirdly, scar tissue from continued pruning tends to restrict sap flow to the new year's shoots, diminishing the yields.

All this may seem self-evident, but what may have been forgotten is the drastic changes that occurred following the phylloxera pandemic. Prior to this, vineyards were seldom (if ever) grubbed up and replanted. (Nowadays vineyards are generally reckoned to become uneconomic in yields after twenty-five to thirty years.)

In pre-phylloxera days, if a vine died, and caused a gap in the vineyard, it was replaced by *provignage*; a long shoot was trained

Figure 8
Barolo soil map

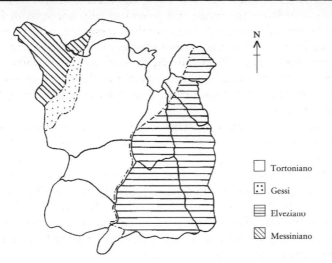

N

☐ Tortoniano

⠒ Gessi

☰ Elveziano

◩ Messiniano

Table 4
Soils found in the Barolo region (classified by colour)

Colour	Soil
White	Calcareous soil with sandstone or freestone, best for Moscato grapes.
Pale whitish-yellow	Elveziano soil, predominant in the Barbaresco region.
Yellow	Sandy soil
Brown	Podsolic profile
Grey-brown	Soil most suitable for the Dolcetto grape
Grey	Tufa subsoil

NOTES

1 The yellow soil described above appears to correspond to the Astiano levels, and may be related to 'les sables jaunes astiens' found in the Costières de Nîmes appellation.
2 Dr. Renato Ratti related the Tortoniano and Messiniano soils (shown on the Barolo soil map) to Piacenziano levels, which may be compared with 'les marnes bleues plaisanciennes' of the Costières de Nîmes, since the name Piacenza in Italian is translated in French into Plaisance.
3 The Astiano soils take their name from Asti, where the Spumante and Moscato Naturale come from. Tortoniano soils take their name from Tortona in the province of Alessandria.
4 The Gesso soils (on the Barolo soil map) with their gypsum connotation should be compared with the 'Yeso' gypsums found just outside the Sherry area and used for plastering the grapes in sherry-making.

into its place from a neighbouring vine, layered into the soil, and in due course, when well rooted and established, became the replacement vine in the row. (You may still see this occurring in old vineyards, but the layered vine will be susceptible to phylloxera infection.)

In time (in general, after about twenty-five years), the yields from the original vines would fall to uneconomic levels, and another form of *provignage* could be undertaken. A large hole would be dug alongside the old vine, the old vine-stock would be forced down into this hole, and buried; the flexible year's shoots would be twisted upwards to emerge from the ground, and staked to provide replacement vines. This twisting of the shoots would torsion the cambium layer, and encourage the formation of adventitious roots. These would provide new sap-flow for the grapes, while the reserves in the old underground stock could ensure continuity of quality. Sometimes, the hole in the ground would only be partly filled for the first year, to encourage the growth of the new shoots, and the provident grower might plant a catch-crop of beans and garlic on the piles of earth.

Alongside these advantages of this form of *provignage*, there were some disadvantages. Cultivating the soil with your mattock, your shoulder could be severely jolted when you hit the vine-stock buried by your grandfather! And you ended up with twice as many vines per hectare as you started with.

You could avoid the second problem if you chopped off one of the arms of the old vine before burying it. If you were renewing a whole vineyard, you would find that you had a pile of pieces of vine, each consisting of a lump of ancient vine, and the pruned-down young shoot emerging from it. This was called a *chapon*, since it looked a little like a trussed capon.

In those days, if you wanted to plant a new vineyard, you did not need to graft a noble scion onto a phylloxera-resistant rootstock (as now), and then plant the slender slip into the soil and wait two or three years for your first decent crop. Instead, you took your *chapons* to a running brook and immersed them for a week or two, until they were swollen and engorged. You then used them to plant up a new vineyard, relying on the inherent quality in the lump of old vinestock to give a flying start to quality production.

BORDEAUX AND BURGUNDY

When that brilliant taster, Ronald Avery, of Bristol (or was it André L. Simon?), was asked, 'Have you ever mistaken a burgundy for a claret?', he paused, and then replied, 'Not since lunch-time.' Having myself been in a quandary on such a question, and having often failed to pick up the hoped-for clues on the nose, I pondered long and often whether there was in fact any essential difference in nature between the red wines of these two great wine districts.

I believe I was given an indication of one possible explanation, when Louis Vallet, of Gevrey Chambertin, stated his opinion that a top red burgundy could not really express its true nature unless it had an alcoholic strength of at least 13 degrees, hence the prevalence of chaptalization. But I knew that many of the top clarets were comparatively low in alcohol, and might well be only 12 to 12.5 degrees in strength. Then I found examples of Bordeaux alcohol-to-extract ratios in Ribéreau-Gayon's textbook. When I compared them with similar ratios for top red burgundies, the explanation seemed to be that the 'body' of clarets depended more on extract, whereas the weight and richness of burgundies relied more on the alcohol.

WINE TEXTURES

'Mouth-feel' is a term sanctified by inclusion in the ISO Sensory Vocabulary, but I still feel somewhat uncomfortable about using it – it seems an ugly word! But the sensations that wine can create in the mouth are very real, and I use them regularly, especially when tasting the red Loire wines. Chinon and Bourgueil are made from the same grape – Cabernet Franc – which I try to identify on the nose from a whiff of new-mown hay; the Italians use the word *erbace* to describe the characteristics of Cabernet Franc. Chinon and Bourgueil do not have any specific differences in strengths, yet their styles are quite separate and distinctive; I find it best to distinguish them on the palate. I have often used the term 'satiny' for fine Chinon wines, because for me, satin has a smoothness and a shine to it, a suppleness and lightness, without being at all thin and filmy. Bourgueil (and particularly Saint-Nicholas-de-Bourgueil) on the other hand, has more depth and texture – without being a heavyweight – so a mature good vintage is for me a more velvety wine.

Louis Vallet introduced me to a term that he used for the most elegant wines of Gevrey-Chambertin (and particularly some of Trapet's Chambertins), which was '*chat*'. The first time I heard him use the term I got entirely the wrong image, since I had recently come across some unsatisfactory German white wines made from the Scheurebe variety, with a whiff of tom-cat! (On the other hand, really ripe Scheurebe grapes can yield a wonderful range of fruit-salad flavours.) The image that Louis Vallet was trying to evoke was the sensation of stroking a cat's back, that sensuous combination of the sleek fur underlain with the supple muscularity beneath. So I have accepted it as a useful addition for my personal note-taking, but remain chary about using it to describe wines to other people.

15

Wine States

SOLID, LIQUID, GAS

When the new wine is bubbling in the fermenting vat, and the cap of pips, skins and grape fragments rises to the surface of the liquid, we are presented with examples of the classic three states of matter: solid, liquid and gas. We are, of course, familiar with them in the form of ice, water and steam. And we know that we can change ice to water, and water to steam, by applying energy in the form of heat, and change them back again by subtracting energy, i.e. cooling.

This should make us cast our minds back to that earlier part of the year, when sunshine and warmth were making the vine fructify, and energy in the form of sunshine was activating photosynthesis in the plant, combining minerals and water from the soil with carbon dioxide gas in the air, and creating organic compounds for plant growth and grape production. We harvest these organic compounds in the form of grapes; part is in nitrogenous compounds of the grape cells and structure, part in the organic acids in the juice, and part is stored as carbohydrates: starches are the earlier forms of the energy stores, up to the change of colour of the grapes – the *véraison* – and thereafter we find dextrins and sugars. We may also find glycerine, formed by *Botrytis* moulds during noble rot.

The sugar energy goes into the wine, either as alcohol, or residual sugar, and there may be more glycerine traces from one of the fermentation stages. The dextrins and glycerine give us mouth sensations of fullness and flow. We absorb the alcohols and residual sugars into our bodies as carbohydrate energy. Thus the concept

81

that sunshine energy is transmitted to us through the vine and the grape, via the vat, the bottle and the wineglass, is not just a flight of poetic fantasy, but a logical sequence, traceable by science.

'BUBBLY'

Carbon dioxide gas is soluble in water, and the quantity that can be dissolved is in proportion to the temperature. Hence you make better soda water if you put well-chilled water into your soda-making machine. The best champagne cellars are in the *crayères* (the vaults and galleries hewn out of the chalk), which allow the development and maturing of the wine by maintaining a constant temperature of 12°C at a depth of 40 feet.

Over the years a whole vocabulary has evolved to describe the bubblyness of sparkling wines or the pressure of the carbon dioxide gas in the bottles. One may come across references to 'Grand Mousseux' and 'Mousseux', distinguishing the amount of gas in the bottles and hence the quality of the *mousse*. 'Crémant' used to typify the semi-sparkling champagnes where the very fine bubbles creamed over the tongue and filled the mouth with pleasurable sensation; now it is more usually found describing the sparkling wines of other regions, as in 'Crémant d'Alsace' or 'Crémant de Bourgogne'.

Semi-sparkling wines are now more usually termed *pétillant* in French, *spritzig* in German, or *frizzante* in Italian, as in the low-strength bubblies of Lambrusco. These semi-sparkling wines may have retained the natural fermentation bubbles by having been filtered and bottled with counter-pressure CO_2 from gas cylinders, but in some cases they may simply have been injected with bottled gas.

Sometimes a wine may contain traces of CO_2 that are so well dissolved that they are not visibly bubbly. My French cousin told me that he thought that such dissolved CO_2 could make a wine taste less dry; I have not found anything about this in any text-books, nor had any opportunity of testing it experimentally. Also I have been told that CO_2 can complex with sugars in a wine, making the gas remain in solution, and not come bubbling out. Could these two things be linked? In cases where I may have suspected such minutely dissolved CO_2 in a wine, I have discovered a useful trick: I run the wine *under* my tongue! It seems that I can sense a tickly feeling under the tongue, which distinguishes itself from the general acidity sensations in the rest of the mouth which might have been masking any dissolved CO_2.

'HENRY'S LAW'

Whenever I mention Henry's Law to people, a strange phenomenon occurs: a glazed look comes into their eyes, and if they admit to having heard of it they never seem to be able to place it exactly. For years I had not managed to trace an authoritative definition of it in the literature. I am now informed that it says that: 'The amount of gas absorbed by a given volume of a liquid at a given temperature is directly proportional to the pressure of the gas.' In wine-making and wine-maturing practice its effect seems to be that a gas at greater pressure will inhibit the action of a gas at lesser pressure.

I came across an eminently practical use of it when Michel Rémon was making an early bottling of the new vintage of Chablis. The wine had only just finished its malolactic fermentation, and was full of dissolved carbon dioxide gas. In the olden days there were one or two different ways of dealing with this: rousing the casks, or racking the wine, and, more unusually, giving the wine a 'silica sand fining'. For this, you took a quantity of well-washed sharp river sand, put it into the cask and stirred it well around. The angular granules brought the gas out of solution, and started it bubbling to the surface. Some glasses, specially designed for sparkling wines, used to have a small cross or star etched into the bottom of the bowl, and you could see the strings of bubbles arising from the sharp edges of the cuts.

But Michel Rémon had a much more up-to-date and elegant method: into the pipe-line between the vat of Chablis and the bottling plant, he had installed a 'gizmo' that introduced nitrogen gas under pressure into the wine as it flowed along. I think there was a venturi tube to accelerate the flow as the nitrogen was introduced. The nitrogen, under pressure (or maybe nitrogen oxide impurities in the gas), brought the carbon dioxide gas out of solution from the wine (apparently from the corollary to Henry's Law), and it bubbled out into the air as the bottles were filled.

And the nitrogen gas was insoluble, so this also bubbled out during the bottling, so that the wine was neatly de-gassed. After all, it is out of character for a Chablis to be *pétillant*.

And I believe that Henry's Law plays a part in keeping champagnes and other sparkling wines fresh and elegant, since the pressure of carbon dioxide gas in the bottles could inhibit oxidation.

INERT GASES

Many wine-makers now use carbon dioxide gas to keep out the air when handling wines, to cut down on oxidation. But it was nearly forty years ago that Jules Chauvet carried out a fascinating series of experiments to compare the effect of various inert gases on the handling of Beaujolais Villages wines in cask, compared with the traditional exposure to air, or the effect of pure oxygen. Apart from the oxygen, carbon dioxide and nitrogen casks, and the control cask (handled traditionally), he let me taste casks of the same wine handled with noble gases, such as argon and neon. It was, of course, a blind tasting, so I did not know which cask was which, but my recollection is that pure oxygen had advanced the maturity of the wine, one of the carbon dioxide casks had a slight 'spritz', both nitrogen casks had the slightest hint of 'cellar mould', and that the casks with the noble gases were the slowest-maturing. The 'cellar mould' note might have occurred because nitrogenous matters can be food for micro-organisms.

I had been used to seeing vats being filled with wine by putting a pipe into the top, and letting the vat fill up, and we relied on sulphur dioxide to protect the wine from oxidation. But Jules Chauvet showed me an elegant alternative way of filling a vat. He opened the door at the bottom of the vat, and sprayed carbon dioxide from a cylinder on to the floor of the vat, so that the bottom of the vat was covered with a layer of 'dry ice'. He closed the door, connected the filling pipe to the drainage connection at the *bottom* of the vat, switched on the pump, and the vat started to fill from the bottom up. The crystals of dry ice floated on the surface of the wine, shielding the wine from any contact with the air in the vat, until the vat was full of wine, right to the top. He then allowed a small quantity of wine, together with the remainder of the dry ice, to overflow from the vat's top connection into a spare container. Thus he had handled this wine without any contact with the air, and with virtually no absorption of CO_2.

SULPHUR

Sulphur is the traditional antioxidant and sterilizing agent used in wine-making. In our cellar-work, after we had emptied and washed out the casks, we always burnt one or two sulphur 'candles' to keep the casks fresh for the next filling. Each 'candle' was a one-inch wide strip of cloth or paper, impregnated with pure sulphur, which you could hang on to a hooked wire; you lit the sulphur, lowered it on the wire into the centre of the cask, and let it burn so that the sulphur fumes filled the cask and killed off any un-wanted micro-organisms.

Julian Jeffs recalls that, when he was in Jerez on one occasion, someone carelessly lowered a sulphur candle into a cask that had contained brandy. He says that the explosion was impressive.

In the 1950s and early 1960s, people in the wine trade were worried about wild yeasts producing secondary fermentation, and quite large quantities of free sulphur were used. A lot of people found that they were unable to drink white wines at that time, because they were allergic to sulphur, and their faces and necks used to get flushed after the first mouthful. It was the free sulphur that was effective against micro-organisms, and was the antioxidant, and any combined sulphur was fairly ineffective. One of the London wine-bottling warehouses had problems with stray beer yeasts from a nearby brewery! Worse still, these prevalent high dosages of sulphur seemed to be breeding sulphur-resistant strains of yeast. Since then, new regulations and improved cellar-work have generally reduced sulphur levels.

Ascorbic acid (Vitamin C), which occurs naturally in wine in small quantities, was suggested as an antioxidant alternative to sulphur, but it seemed to be easily lost in a cellar context, and I was told that it was destroyed by contact with metals. Jules Chauvet worked out that it might be possible to used calculated dosages of SO_2 to protect ascorbic acid, and then the ascorbic acid would permit lower quantities of SO_2.

COMBINED SULPHUR

Too much combined sulphur can make a wine most unattractive. If you find it in the form of mercaptans, or sulphites, you can meet an array of unwelcome or downright unpleasant smells. I tend to classify them in an ascending order of pungency. The lightest and least offensive is like the smell of the wild garlic flower. Then come a range of farmyard smells, up to manure-heap standard. I am not sure whether I put 'burnt rubber' or 'cabbage-water' next. I don't think I have come across sulphuretted hydrogen ('bad eggs') in any of the dodgy wines I have met, but I believe it is possible. Mercaptans seem to be the result of the action of yeasts on sulphur, and can occur in cask. If they can be spotted at an early stage, they are usually volatile, and racking the cask off the lees into a clean cask may cure the fault. But if they are left too long, they are apt to get stuck in the wine, and may be irremediable. I am apt to be rather critical, since I suspect that they may be a sign of carelessness in the cellar. But you should be careful not to confuse farmyard smells (which might indicate faults) with the autumnal leaf-mould aroma, which is a characteristic of Richebourg.

But more usually, sulphur's antioxidant action means that the sulphur molecule picks up extra oxygen, so that it can become SO_3, which I tend to taste as a hard end to the wine, discernible on the palate. I worry about this, since, with ageing, it can develop into sulphurous acid (and even sulphuric acid), and give a very 'hot' end-taste to the older wine. The long-term changes can be expressed with the following formulae:

$$H_2O + SO_3 = H_2SO_3 + O$$
$$H_2SO_3 + [O] = H_2SO_4$$

Although most older textbooks seem to suggest that combined sulphur in wine is irreversible, I have seen an exceptional example of the process having been reversed. Fritz Hallgarten showed a fairly nondescript German wine, from one of the 1930s vintages, at a tasting of old wines in the 1960s. This wine was fresh and crisp, and showed no sign at all of age. It had been salvaged from a 'blitzed' cellar; the building above had been burnt down, and the winebottles had presumably become quite hot, but the firemen's hoses, putting out the blaze, had apparently cooled the wine down again, so that it had effectively been 'flash-pasteurized', thereby 'uncombining' the combined sulphur; the released free sulphur had kept the wine young and fresh, in spite of its calendar years.

16

Wine Aromas

ISO TASTING GLASS

It was in Burgundy that Albert Pochon, an old-style wine-broker, introduced me to some of the finest growers, and taught me to taste and understand classic burgundies, while Jules Chauvet, a skilled Beaujolais wine-grower who was also a Ph.D. scientist with the soul of a poet, passed on to me some of his highly disciplined yet intuitive approach to serious tasting. As mentioned earlier, Jules Chauvet had published his researches into the surface-to-volume ratios in wineglasses, which had led to the development and world-wide acceptance of the ISO tasting glass (see Figure 2, p. 13, and p. 109).

The oft-observed difference in style between a champagne served in the saucer-shaped '*champagne coupe*', and the same wine presented in a tall narrow '*champagne flute*', which was Chauvet's starting-point, can be checked by you if you can get hold of the different-shaped glasses when a bottle of champagne is being opened and served. The aroma from the *flute* may well be fine and elegant, whereas the aroma from the same wine in the *coupe* may seem broader and coarser.

If you can accept, as a working hypothesis, that a wine may present aroma notes to the nose in a time sequence, you may then find that it is sometimes possible, by an effort of will, to evaluate them in slow motion, when they may often seem to be in the following order:

flower-perfumes – fruit-notes – spices – herbs – tannins and wood
notes – soil characteristics – sulphur derivatives – faults

The International Standard Organisation (ISO) Wine Tasting Glass is described as 'a truncated egg', and when correctly filled, the wine describes a perfect hemisphere; the wine-to-air surface is in a logical geometrical relationship to the volume of wine below, and there is sufficient air space above it to allow the aromas to spread, before the sides of the glass curve in to concentrate them for the nose. Its air-surface-to-wine-volume ratio was designed to guard against coarse aromas gaining priority over the finer characteristics.

If you can accept that there might exist a special situation at the interface between wine and air, perhaps we ought to consider whether something similar might occur at the interface between wine and glass. So long as we are thinking in terms of solid and liquid (or liquid and gas in the case of the surface-to-air interface), we are apt to think of the interface as a plane of zero thickness. If however we start thinking at an atomic level, relatively large amounts of space are needed for the orbits of electrons, further complicated, no doubt, by quantum mechanics. If we can also accept that 'Sheffield plate' owes its permanence to the milling pressure causing the molecules of the laminae of copper and silver to mingle at the interface, can something similar be occurring at the interfaces of the wine in the glass?

PRIMARY AND SECONDARY AROMAS

The kind of aromas that you meet in a young wine, the simple fruit and flower notes, for example, are called *primary aromas* by tasters – and very good they can certainly be! But the maturing of a wine, causing changes in its balances and complexing of its characteristics, can produce *secondary aromas*, with new and interesting features. Acids may link with alcohols to create esters, wood tannins can merge with grape tannins, so that spice-notes can emerge on the nose, with perfumed 'Russian leather' *(cuir de russie)*, or sometimes sandalwood, on nose and palate.

SHARP NOTES AND FLAT NOTES

When I was trying to organize my ideas about tasting (which was also the time that I was trying repeatedly to pass the Master of Wine examination), I found that I was often using musical analogies. This was a period when we were importing considerable numbers of wines in cask, and bottling them in bonded warehouses, so that they might be available (if required) for re-export to our overseas customers.

At that time shipping delays were becoming intolerable, and although alternative import routes from France were being tried, casks of wine could take up to five weeks from leaving the producer's cellars, before we had access to them in our London cellars or in the London Bonded Warehouses. And as the casks had to be opened up for Customs and Excise inspection and gauging for dutiable purposes, adventitious spoilage organisms had to be watched for, as well as possible oxidation. So I used to go and taste every cask on arrival, make careful notes and, where necessary, arrange for microscopic examination and laboratory analysis.

This gave me an opportunity to define, for my own satisfaction, a relationship between aroma notes, and spoilage organisms. I already knew that traces of volatile acidity (what the French called 'acéscence') seemed to give a lift to aromas. At that time many proprietors in the parish of Margaux were in the habit of using the *chapeau flottant* method of vinification, with the skins and pips rising to the surface, since the minute hint of volatile acidity that it engendered could, with maturing and esterification, add finesse and subtlety to the high notes of the aroma. By way of contrast, the top châteaux of Pauillac seemed to prefer the *chapeau submergé*, seemingly producing richer, deeper notes. For this method of vinification, a grid was fixed, part way down the fermenting vat, which retained the skins and pips below the surface level of the fermenting must. I was particularly lucky in my training in Bordeaux, since the *contre-maître* (assistant cellar-master) of Château Cos d'Estournel took me on a bicycle ride round the neighbouring cellars and discussed technicalities with his counterparts. So I was shown and told things that may not have been in a regular guided tour.

When tasting the wines that had arrived in the UK after shipment, if the cask I was tasting seemed to have a flattened nose, and a rather bland, broad flavour compared with the other casks, I used to suspect that it might have some lactobacilli in it, and asked for this to be checked under the microscope. It seemed to me that the two kinds of micro-organism (*Lactobacillus* and

Acetobacter) appeared to be rather incompatible, and this seemed borne out by something that Marcel Bichat, our wine-broker who acted for us when we were buying Rhône wines, told me. He said that when he was starting in the wine trade, local people used to buy a small cask of wine from him for their own use. This would be quite a full-bodied wine, of 13 degrees of alcohol or more, and they would immediately bottle off a couple of dozen bottles of it, to mature and be used for special occasions – *sous les fagots*. They then topped the cask up with water, which reduced the strength to 11 or 12 degrees, in other words, the strength for everyday drinking, and then they would draw it off from the tap to go with their meals. The wine was on ullage, with an increasing air space over the wine, but it never turned to vinegar, because a film of lactobacilli developed on the surface, which seemed to protect it. He said that the wine was then not particularly good, but the added water had reduced the cost, and it was by no means undrinkable. But then, the *gros rouge* that everyone drank at that time, made from the prolific variety Aramon des Plaines, was pretty rough stuff.

BOTTLE-SICKNESS AND 'FRETS'

You do not seem to hear about bottle-sickness nearly so often nowadays as we did when I was training. Wine-makers must now be more skilled at controlling it. And the technology has changed. I had to be taught how to tap a hogshead of wine, inserting the spout without drenching myself, and then fill the bottles by hand, for someone else to cork with the old corking machine. However skilful, you could not prevent the wine taking up air, and this sudden addition of oxygen inevitably produced a reaction in the wine, manifesting itself as 'bottle-sickness'. Several weeks might be needed before the wine would settle down, and regain its quality, after this period when it appeared flat and without much aroma, and with sharp edges showing on the palate.

Another temporary set-back still occurs in the wine, when it has been fined and racked, although the effect will be diminished if the racking is carried out under an inert gas. And differences in the porosity and grain of cask-staves may cause appreciable differences from cask to cask in a cellar, hence the need to carry out an 'equalization' vatting before bottling. More unusually, years ago I had supplied several casks of wine to a customer for his own bottling; he had fined the wine (as was then customary), but called me in because one cask had not fallen bright. On tasting, we could find nothing wrong, but I noticed one of the cellar candles flickering. By moving the candles around, we were able to discover a draught from a door at the other cellar-end, which impinged on this single cask. So we protected the cask by 'rugging it up' with sacks, and within the week the wine was bright and fit to bottle.

Another oddity is what cellarmen and growers used to call the spring and autumn 'frets'. They used to claim that when the sap was rising in the vines, the wines in the cellar – both in cask and even in bottle – would 'fret' and go out of condition. And when the wines in vat were fermenting in the autumn, wines in bottle would similarly go out of condition. I may have observed an autumn fret when Viv Armstrong, of the City wine merchants Mayor Sworder & Co., asked me to taste a bottle of red Domaine de la Romanée Conti burgundy that he was not happy about. As it was then the autumn equinox, we agreed to put the trouble down to 'autumn fret'. Indeed, a fortnight or so later he reported that the wine was tasting quite splendid again. But of course it might have just been the odd 'rogue' bottle.

The question of spring and autumn frets was then of sufficient interest for a senior member of the wine trade (it may have been Stanley Dennis), to write to the current Astronomer Royal to seek his opinions. I understood his reply to have been that cosmic radiation usually peaked at the equinoxes, and he recommended (as an experiment) that special bottlings should be carried out, with half of each bottling binned normally, and the bottles of the other half wrapped in lead foil before binning. Tastings after five or ten years might provide experimental proof of the effect of cosmic radiation on wine development. As far as I know, these experiments have never (regrettably) been carried out, so we still do not know. But then, of course, for centuries we have been putting wines into dark underground cellars to protect them against actinic rays. On the other hand, I have recently seen foil-wrapped bottles of château Sauternes, with the château labels *over* the foil, apparently to prevent premature ageing.

17

Wine Words

WINE JARGON

I feel a twinge of concern whenever I read of a Chardonnay white wine being described as 'buttery'. This is an accepted shorthand note for the impression given by wines from this particular grape variety. Nevertheless I cannot help wondering what exactly is intended by the word. Is there a herbal note on the nose that I seem to miss, which should recall the lush meadows on which the cattle had grazed? Or does this grape retain a hint of yoghurt from a malolactic fermentation, matching the slightly different smell of the white butters? Or is it about a creamy sensation in the mouth as butter spreads across the tongue ('butter wouldn't melt in his mouth'), or from the way butter can coat the palate? When, by the way, did you last eat a slice of bread-and-butter upside down, so that the butter was against the tongue, and the bread was touching the roof of the mouth?

To a lesser extent, the same may apply to 'blackberry'. It is one of the accepted fruit-notes, though not as popular as 'blackcurrant', which is an accepted indentifier for Cabernet Sauvignon. I am concerned at a certain lack of precision. There is a world of difference between the pippy, slightly tart yet refreshing wild blackberry, or bramble, with its firm tannins, and the luscious ripe cultivated blackberry, with its sweet juiciness.

When giving tutored tastings, I often supply the students with a tasting *aide-mémoire* (see Figure 9), which may help to bring into focus perceptions that had previously been only half-identified. But if a student should find 'soft fruits' in a wine, I would then want it to be narrowed, between strawberries, raspberries, mulberries,

Figure 9
Tasting *aide-mémoire*

Appearance

Colour   purplish • ruby • red • brick-red • brownish
rosé • salmon • pale pink • blush
greeny-white • water-white • pale
yellow • golden-yellow • deep gold • brownish

Richness   depth of colour • fullness of flow

Brilliance   limpid • hazy • cloudy • piecy

Nose

Flowery   spring flowers • summer flowers • potpourri

Fruity   soft fruits • stone fruits • apples and pears

Spicy   vanilla • cinnamon • peppery • etc

Herbs   thyme • rosemary • bay • etc

Soils   flinty • slatey • smoky • earthy • etc

Yeasty   or Winey (vinosity) or Volatile (acetic)

Palate

Taste-buds   sweet • acid • (bitter) • (salty)

Mouth-feel   rough/smooth • round/sharp • thin/full • warmth/coolness
flow • length

Remarks   too young • young and fresh • ready to drink
better in x years • mature • will keep for y years
over the top • worn out

loganberries, blackberries, blackcurrants, redcurrants, white-currants, gooseberries. And if strawberries were then selected, I would pose the choice between cultivated strawberries and wild strawberries!

When tasting cask samples of Château Ausone, that great St Emilion red wine, I often used to get the delicious aroma of wild strawberries – the French *fraises des bois*; on the other hand, very old bottles of Château Ausone used to remind me of aromatic cedarwood.

CLICHÉS AND REAL PERCEPTIONS

Clichés and stereotypes have become divorced from their printers' origins, where they were a means of recreating at will images and phrases with accuracy and precision. Even if they may have acquired pejorative overtones, one ought to recognize their value as a means of communication. The wine-taster should accept another's use of jargon or clichés with courtesy and understanding, but you should, of course, try to avoid slapdash wording and imprecision when describing wines yourself.

The taster should try to relate every word to personal experience. If you would like to use the word 'steely', for example, why not put a piece of steel into your mouth, note the sensations and the taste, and then sniff the steel afterwards. It should naturally be a piece of ordinary steel, since wine words are apt to predate the invention of stainless steel. In those earlier days, if you ate fish with a steel knife, the contact turned the knife black, and imparted a metallic taste to the food. Hence the introduction of special silver fish-knives and forks. However, it is said that the British Royal Family retain a tradition of eating fish with two silver forks, which would also be a way of avoiding the steely taste. And I suspect that the cookbooks that tell you to tear your lettuce, rather than cutting it up with a knife, may be harking back to the time that ordinary steel knives were blackened likewise by contact with lettuce juice, and this again predates the introduction of stainless steel.

Many years ago, I was due to give a tutored tasting on Bordeaux wines, and one of the samples was a typically 'gun-flint' white Graves, a Château Carbonnieux of fairly recent vintage. It occurred to me that I had not handled a flintlock pistol since I was a child, when I had unexpectedly found one hidden in a Sussex barn. At the time of that lecture I was still a cigarette-smoker, so I looked out an empty cigarette lighter, and snapped it several times, sniffing the spark. It was nothing like anything I had ever come across in a white Graves, so I decided to make a point in my lecture, warning against using outdated jargon phrases. To dramatize the point, I went to a gunsmith's, and hired a Tower Pistol, with its flintlock in full working order, but of course without primer, powder or shot. When the time came for the students to smell and taste the Château Carbonnieux, I snapped the lock of the pistol under the nose of each student in turn, producing an impressive spark. I had been surprised to find that the smell from a cigarette-lighter flint was nothing like the much stronger whiff from a flintlock firearm, and the consensus view of the class was that the old phrase was still valid, and that 'gun-flint' was the most precise description of the aroma of that vintage of Château Carbonnieux, and probably of dry white Graves in general.

Nowadays, when I come across some of the more high-flown description of wines in the media, I feel a twinge of guilt: could I be held responsible for all these flowery phrases? Inspired by Jules Chauvet's tasting tuition, I had written an article for a wine magazine, entitled 'The Wine-Lover's Perfumed Garden'. In it, I had suggested plants that one might grow in one's garden, in order to 'tune up' the nose for recognition of the various aroma-notes I had come across in wines of the 1959 and 1961 vintages. In particular, I had been astounded by a 1961 Morgon Le Py; when the proprietress had sprung the cask open with two smart raps of the 'flogger' mallet on either side of the bung, the whole cellar had been filled with the scent of violets. It is experiences like that which reward and encourage one's love of wine.

18

Tasting Skills

TASTING DURING FERMENTATION

Wine-growers have often told me that it is easier to taste the unfermented grape must and gauge the possible quality of the eventual wine than to taste while the wine is still fermenting. Unfortunately, no one has ever taught me the art of tasting grape-must, so I am unable to comment.

I have however been given many opportunities of tasting from vats and casks before they have been racked at the end of fermentation. I would certainly not claim this to be a pleasurable experience, with a conglomeration of yeasty notes and off-flavours, pasty sensations on the palate, and often a variety of sulphur-stinks!

There are, however, several tricks to help one weave one's way through this labyrinth. First of all, one needs plenty of saliva in the mouth, and to chew away at the wine, in order to mix the saliva well in. This starts to neutralize some of the aggressive acids (see 'The oral acid test', pp. 20–21, which we hope will be somewhat abated during maturation.

Next, the alkalinity of the saliva should take quite a few of the anthocyanins past the isoelectric point of tannin (see pp. 56–57), so that they flocculate and come out of solution, reducing the bitter notes which can mask the eventual fruit of the wine. By pressing the tongue against the palate, one can feel a grittiness from the tannin particles.

Air should now be bubbled through the mouthful of wine, to try to oxidize some of the aromas and flavours, which have previously been locked within the reductive state of the young wine (see Chapter 22 in Part II, p. 112).

There still remain the problems of the off-flavours and odd aromas arising from the fermentation process. This is where the taster's will-power is put to the test. One must deliberately taste for, and concentrate in turn on, each and every temporary fault in the wine. One must hold them all in one's attention, and then taste *through* them, to perceive what lies behind.

I have found it a useful analogy to imagine that I am driving at night in a rainstorm. I know that there are raindrops everywhere, and that the windscreen wipers are constantly passing in front of my line of vision. But I also know that I can (and must) concentrate on the road ahead; that is my focus of attention. If one can persuade the brain to accept this trick of tasting *through* any fermentation faults, one may be able to visualize the incipient qualities that may eventually come in the wine.

Needless to say, one has to learn which are temporary faults that will disappear when fermentation ends and the wine is racked. One must be taught what may be defects that can persist, and whether they may be rectified. And finally, one must know how to identify an incorrigible wine that should be rejected. This is not an easy process, and I am always cautious about borderline cases. Nevertheless, there is great satisfaction in recognizing a splendid wine before competitors can get their hands on it.

TONE-DEAFNESS

One occasionally comes across people who are not stone-deaf, but are unable to distinguish tonalities; their attempts to sing can be excruciating! We are also quite aware of the incidence of colour-blindness (Daltonism), which may vary in degree. What is less well known is that some unfortunate people are unable to smell; this is recorded in the ISO sensory vocabulary as 'anosmia'. (Inability to taste is 'ageusia'.) Although total anosmia is rare, I believe that partial anosmia may be occurring in the population, yet seldom recognized. While I have proved to be a generally competent taster, I have discovered that I have partial anosmia, in the range of 'corkiness' and 'dry-woodiness'. The 'dry-wood' taste is caused by a faulty stave in a cask, and coopers used to blame it on cellar-staff carelessness in failing to clean out and sterilize a barrel after emptying it. Corkiness is likewise due to an infection in the bark of the cork-oak tree from which the cork was cut. The nearest I can get to describing 'corkiness' is the slightly acrid smell of an empty house that has suffered from dry-rot. If I think that I can sense it, I then double-check with the palate, since I am more sensitive to the parching dryness on the palate that may accompany it. If I find this, I usually ask someone else to taste and confirm my suspicions.

This ability (or inability) to taste things involves what the ISO vocabulary defines as 'thresholds'. The vocabulary defines a number of 'thresholds', such as the moment when you know you can taste something, but cannot say what it is; again, the point when it is stronger, and you can identify the characteristic; the range through which you can evaluate progressive differences in strength; and then the moment when the palate is so numb that you cannot say whether there is any difference in this overwhelming sensation.

I suspect that one's personal thresholds can vary, according to one's state of health or tiredness. Traditionally, tea-tasters started the day by tasting a standard blend; if it tasted different from usual, their own acuity was suspect, and they might refrain from doing any important tastings. What I am uncertain about, is the degree (if any) to which one's thresholds may be conditioned. When I came into the trade, the wine-growers of the Margaux district (as has been mentioned) traditionally fermented their clarets with a floating cap which created a trace of volatile acidity, with the intention that this should later esterify and lift the aromas. Alan Sichel, a pillar of the UK wine trade but based in Margaux, had from time to time marketed wines with noticeable volatile acidity, and I have often wondered whether he might have been conditioned by the Margaux environment, so that his threshold for volatility had changed.

I learnt quite a lot about thresholds when I was running Maurice Meyer Ltd, a company that specialized in a wide range of spirits and liqueurs; Maurice Meyer was apparently the first person to import vodkas into the UK in any quantity. I therefore set about reconstituting the recipe for 'red vodka', a flavoured vodka that had been quite widespread in the southern regions of the Russian

Empire, and which had been made and dispensed privately in Paris by G.I. Gurdjieff. In the process I discovered quite a number of things about the many ways in which vodka had been made in the past. In round terms, vodka had been made from almost any fermentable surpluses that could then be distilled into a (relatively) pure alcohol. Unfortunately, due to dubious raw materials and 'bathtub hooch' distilling, a wide variety of recipes were evolved to counter the wet-socks smells and eliminate the deleterious fusel oils. Hence you found Zubrovka flavoured with bison grass, and Starka cask-matured with apple leaves. I came across a witches'-brew German recipe for vodka, which we tried out of curiosity, using the only thing we had to hand – a bottle of Plymouth Gin! Half-way through the process, the gin turned black, but after we had filtered it, it was clear and clean-flavoured, a vodka with no trace of Plymouth aromatics and botanicals. It was, of course, Pierre Smirnoff who developed the simple technique of filtering the spirit through activated charcoal to produce clean and neutral vodka.

With quite a large number of recipes involving a wide variety of ingredients, I was curious why some of them were included; according to the herbalists, many seemed to have digestive or appetite-stimulating qualities. So I tried to include as many of them as possible. But this was where thresholds came into play. I diluted each ingredient *below* the recognition threshold, but well above the perception threshold, so that, although you knew there was something there that you could taste, you could not really identify it. With the variety of ingredients, some of which had similarities, you could know, however, that you were tasting something interesting and pleasurable. People kept finding different aromas and flavours that in fact were not there as ingredients; they each seemed to be half-tasting different groups of ingredients. However, when we were working on the red vodka recipe, we found that we could not taste for very long, not because of any palate-fatigue, but because we became so hungry, and had to go home for our suppers. As a pre-prandial drink, it certainly worked. And people who had tasted Gurdjieff's red vodka and were asked to compare my version, made the general comment that Gurdjieff's was more direct and rustic, but that mine was more commercial. Regrettably, it never really made it in the market-place, partly a victim of successive rises in the rate of excise duty on spirits.

19

Other People's Tastes

BLANDNESS VERSUS CHARACTER

Heat causes liquid to evaporate, so the sunshine of a good vintage can reduce the proportion of the grape liquid and concentrate the juice. Providing the vine-roots have been extracting good elements from the soil or interesting minerals from the subsoil, these characteristics can be concentrated, first by the quality of the weather during the growing season, and also by the vintner's skills during wine-making.

Strong characteristics may appeal very much to some people, yet be unattractive to others. One of the challenges to the professional wine-taster is to distance himself or herself from such personal choices, and to try to assess how others may judge them.

In between the extremes of wine styles marked by strong characteristics, one can find more neutral wines to which the majority of the population will not be averse. Such wines may well be the kind that are chosen for mass-marketing. This is the field where soundly crafted blandness may reign supreme.

VINTAGE CHARTISMS

The 1950s and 1960s saw the emergence of new wine-drinkers, encouraged by common-sense wine writers like Raymond Postgate. These wine-drinkers relied on the ubiquitous Food and Wine Society vintage chart, with its single-figure scale of 0 to 7. We felt that this was very limiting, since it ignored the recognized fact that some good wines can be made in unsatisfactory years, and some bad wines can occur in good years. Our 'Wineograph Chart' (in its various editions) would be (we hoped) the wine chart to end all wines charts, since it suggested wines over a range of prices, to go with different foods (not just the totemic 'white wine with fish, red wine with meat'). The Wineograph Vintage Chart gave the *spread* of quality to be expected in any particular year and wine district, on a scale of 0 to 10. This allowed us to distinguish an excellent year (say, 8–10), where nearly all the wines were good, from an uneven year (say, 4–8), when some wines could be very good, yet others were to be avoided.

Since those long-forgotten days, a number of factors have changed. Improvements in wine-making and quality control have reduced the spread, so that the single-figure vintage chart now makes more sense. New World wines, which now need to be included, seem less influenced by vagaries of sunshine and weather. Perhaps more important still, wine lists and wine labels have become much more informative, while maturing times, for all except the top wines, seem to be shortening.

WINE AND FOOD: COMPARE AND CONTRAST

When I was talking to students about the wide variety of wine styles to be found in the Loire valley, with the white wines ranging from light, crisp and dry, to wonderful rich sweet wines, I used to try to make them use their wine-tasting imagination. Starting with their ready agreement to 'white wine with fish', and taking the sole as the classic white fish, I then reminded them of some of the traditional recipes for preparing sole. What kind of wines would you offer if the sole was simply grilled, and served with lemon and parsley; if it was fried in butter; with a cheese sauce (Mornay); or cooked in wine, and garnished with halved and seeded muscatel grapes (Véronique)? I had probably been showing them (among others) a light crisp Muscadet, made from the grape that originated as the little-regarded Melon de Bourgogne, and only came into its own when translated towards the mouth of the Loire, and matched to the seafoods of the Brittany coast; a dry Pouilly Blanc Fumé, from Sauvignon Blanc grapes grown on the *argilo-calcaire* soils around Les Loges; a full and fruity dry Vouvray, made from Chenin Blanc grapes grown on oölithic limestone subsoil; and one of the sweeter Chenin Blanc wines from the Coteaux du Layon.

Matching food and wine can be fun, but contrasting food and wine can be more challenging and stimulating. Louis Vallet used to serve braised chicory (*endive*) as a side-dish to red meat when serving fine red burgundy; he argued that the braising carameliz-ation partnered the roasting flavours of the meat, while the slightly bitter tang of the vegetable made the red wine taste sweeter.

My father was happy to match a full burgundy or Rhône red wine with roast goose; but more imaginatively, he recommended a fine Moselle with roast goose, since the high acidity would help to cut through the rich fat flavours, and help digestion. His other – even more iconoclastic – suggestion was a fine malt whisky with the goose!

THEME AND VARIATIONS

Research is going on all the time into tasting in all its aspects, to discover the common factors in the way we react to flavour and aroma. But it is also making clear the wide variations in individual responses. Each of us has a different metabolism, which will influ-ence our tastes – our likes and dislikes. And these are not constant. Pregnancy can strongly affect a woman's tastes, so that she may suddenly find that she cannot abide tea or coffee. No one's tastes are constant, so that, as people grow older, they may develop a taste for dry wines which they did not like in their youth, when (maybe) physical activity and a need for extra calories might have induced a taste for sweeter wines.

That is one of the joys of wine. It provides a constant challenge and stimulus, with new wine appearing each year. We need to reassess, not only each wine as it matures, but our own selves as tasters, as we gain experience or age.

And when we entertain friends, we should study their tastes and, by an effort of the imagination, try to find the combination of food and wine that will make them smile and sparkle.

From among the multiplicity of wines around the world, may we have the skill and good fortune to find those that may match the diversity of human types. When I was a wine-shipper, I used to comfort myself with the thought that if everyone had the same tastes, we would not sell half our wines.

20

Concluding

===

WINE FANTASIA

Since we started our search for a logical thread through the labyrinth of wines, we have been diverted on to some of the wilder shores of speculation and imagination. This may be excusable if we recall that through the ages wine-making was an art, or craft, and only since Pasteur has science become involved.

From ancient times wine has had magical and religious overtones, and you can still find wine-growers who prune, harvest or bottle according to the phases of the moon. Remember also that until relatively recent times, the pruning or harvesting knife was the sickle-shape of the new moon.

So I would be saddened if too much emphasis on science and logic were to stifle wine's poetry, and reduce it to the prosaic. May I therefore quote to you one of my favourite pieces of prose from a poet, taken from a letter that John Keats wrote to George and Georgina Keats on 19th February 1819:

> – now, I like Claret, whenever I can have Claret I must drink it. 't is the only palate affair that I am at all sensual in,
> Would it not be a good Speck to send you some vine-roots could it be done? I'll enquire
> If you could make some wine like Claret to drink on summer evenings in an arbour! For really 't is so fine
> it fills the mouth one's mouth with a gushing freshness, then goes down cool and feverless.
> then you do not feel it quarelling with your liver
> no it is rather a Peace maker and lies as quiet as it did in the grape

then it is as fragrant as the Queen Bee; and the more ethereal Part of it mounts into the brain, not assaulting the cerebral apartments, like a bully in a bad house seeking after his trul, and hurrying from door to door bouncing against the wai[n]stcoat; but rather walks like Aladin about his own enchanted palace, so gently that you do not feel his step.

II
PRACTISING TASTING

21

Starting-points

―――――

TASTING SAMPLES

In general, it is best to select wines for your tasting comparisons in similar price brackets. If there is a choice, you may learn more with wines from single vineyards, or reputable growers, rather than commercial or branded wines. If in doubt, ask for advice from a knowledgeable wine merchant or reliable supplier.

TASTING-GLASSES

Since different-shaped glasses are believed to bring out different characteristics in wines, you should use the same shapes and sizes of glasses throughout a tasting session. The International Tasting Glass (see Figure 2, p. 13, and p. 88) has been approved for wine-tasting by the International Standards Organisation (ISO), so it may be a preferred choice if available. (There is also a little-used ISO-approved glass for spirits.) Otherwise, clean clear glasses of reasonable size may be used. The tulip shape has its merits, and the Elgin glass its demerits; glass manufacturers such as Riedel are developing suites of glasses to enhance the quality of specific wines, and these may be a preferred choice when tasting a range of these wines. The wineglass stem helps to keep a cigarette-smoker's fingers away from the nose, so tumblers are seldom used; it is not easy to swirl a wine around in them. And many people find a thick rim on a glass unattractive, putting heavy cut-glass at a disadvantage.

Traces of detergents may affect the surface tension of the wines being tasted; so, if detergents have to be used, the glasses should then be well rinsed. Since traces of detergents sometimes seem to cling to glasses, I like to wash wineglasses in hot water with some washing soda, rinse them with fresh hot water, and then drain them. New glass-polishing cloths often contain a dressing to make them appear crisp and well ironed; such cloths should be washed out and dried before use. When glass-cloths have been laundered, check that they do not reek of perfumed laundry powder. And if glasses have been left to drain upside-down, check that they have not been tainted from paper or cloth that they have been standing on. Always sniff an empty glass before using it.

TASTING PANELS

As individuals' tasting abilities and perceptions may vary so widely, the ISO has published a Methodology for Sensory Analysis, suggesting the number of tasters (whom they refer to as 'assessors') required in order to iron out personal quirks and quiddities, and produce statistically valid results. For marketing purposes, you might need a hundred or more ordinary folk ('naïve assessors'), whereas for quality control a dozen or so trained tasters ('selected assessors') could suffice, or even only one or two 'expert assessors' in certain cases.

You may find it helpful to taste alongside others, and I have found much to learn on tasting panels. The presence of others can be very stimulating, but may, however, prove distracting. Since wine-tasting can demand considerable concentration, there may well be times when it is preferable to taste alone. Some people are apt to taste fast, and may become impatient if you take your time to seek beyond the obvious.

TASTING RECORDS

Training the memory is an important part of wine-tasting, but it would be unwise to rely too much upon memory, and fail to make a record that you might later need, either to refresh the memory or for comparison purposes.

It is important to record primarily what you yourself perceive, and whatever you may deduce from your perceptions, even if you may be missing something or making erroneous deductions. Only

then should you record other views, and record possible correc-
tions. Self-deception is all too easy!

For more detailed suggestions about the ways in which you
might wish to keep your tasting records, see Chapter 31, p. 155.

KEEP PRACTISING

Wine-tasting is a skill, and few people, however talented, can do
it by the light of nature. One can always learn more from other
tasters, whose backgrounds may yield special enlightenments. But
tasting skills also need to be well burnished. You need to taste as
often as you can.

When I was taking the Master of Wine examination, I passed
the Theory section straight away; fortunately the paper covered
subjects of which I had practical experience, and the questions fell
into my lap. But I kept failing the Practical examination. Finally,
in desperation, I got a young member of our staff to go out and
buy bottles of the kind of wines that I did not come across in our
wine-shipping tastings – for example, Madeiras, commercial
brands of ports and sherries, branded table wines. Every morning,
for three months, he set out ten samples for me to taste blind,
until I was achieving a respectable success rate. Then I passed the
examination, thank goodness.

TASTING OR SOCIAL DRINKING

Wine is an important social lubricant, and is there to be enjoyed
in company and often with food. The kind of thinking that may
be demanded in a serious tasting session can be a conversation-
stopper if voiced on such occasions. But you may well wish to
build up a store of experience about the ways that wines can seem
different when they are presented in varying circumstances, or
with different dishes. It may be possible to switch off the critical
faculty from the conscious mind when enjoying wine in a social
situation, while still tucking away useful memories into the back
of your mind.

22

How Wines Change: Oxido-reduction

SHERRY DEVELOPMENT AND CLASSIFICATION

Sherry is a Spanish white wine, made from white grapes, and it is the way it behaves and is handled after the first fermentation has finished that makes it different from white table wines. Originally, a tumultuous fermentation bubbled up through the bungs of the casks (butts), and when it subsided, it left an air space (ullage) above the wine, and some of the casks developed a film of yeast (*flor*) on the surface. This film of yeast shields the wines from the air, and the yeasts strip the underlying wine of oxygen, so that they remain in a reductive condition, pale in colour, fine and fresh-tasting, hence they were named '*finos*'. It is curious that one of the few other wines that were made like this was the 'Vin Jaune' of the Jura region of France; for about sixty years the Spanish Crown owned lands in that area! And I have tasted a wine, similar to a fino sherry, made in the south of Portugal not far from the Spanish frontier.

Other casks of the new sherry, on ullage with a similar air space, do not have a film of yeast, so the wines oxidize as they mature, and their different aromatic qualities led to their being named '*olorosos*'. Although some of the richer olorosos gain their character from the other sherry grape (Pedro Ximénez), which is one of the two principal grapes used to make the sweetening wines called '*dulces*', dry olorosos are basically made from the predominant Palomino sherry grape, as are fino sherries.

The casks of new wines had traditionally been marked with a single stroke (*raya*), and when the skilled tasters assessed the new wines they modified the mark of the lighter fino-style wines with a tick, converting it to a palm-leaf (*palma*), while fuller-flavoured casks destined for olorosos had an 'o' impressed over the *raya*, producing the oloroso mark ø. Wines of an in-between style, with the finesse of a fino and the body of an oloroso, received a horizontal stroke across the *raya*, implying a broken stick, hence Palo Cortado ⨍. Neutral wines destined for blending and producing the lower-value sherries remained as Rayas /.

Other styles can be developed, either by maturing, blending, sweetening or colouring (see Figures 10, 11 and 12).

DRY FINO/DRY OLOROSO

This contrast tasting should show the aroma differences between a fino wine developed in a reducing situation, and the oxidizing development of the oloroso. If you accept the concept of a gamut of aromas, you may find on the nose that the fino has higher notes, while the oloroso produces deeper tones. In the mouth, the fino may show a crisper character, and the oloroso a fuller, broader style.

DRY FINO/DRY MANZANILLA

The distinction between Manzanilla and fino sherry is that Manzanilla has been matured by the seaside; it should therefore have taken up a special character from the spindrift-influenced air of the shore. Some Jerezanos aver that you can take a young fino from the Jerez area, store it at Sanlúcar de Barrameda, and that it can turn into a Manzanilla; moreover, they claim that a Manzanilla taken from the seaside and matured in Jerez cellars can lose its original character, and become a fino. As a result, Spanish Wine Law made a distinction between *zona de producción* and *zona de crianza* – where the wine was made, and where it was matured.

It also seems that the moderating effect of the sea and the River Guadalquivir on the Sanlúcar microclimate can allow the *flor* film to continue to grow throughout the year, giving continuing protection against oxidation, while in other parts of the region the *flor* may die off and then re-grow.

One of the characteristics of sherries is that the *flor* prevents them from being racked off the lees produced by the yeast-film, so

Figure 10
Sherry development and classification

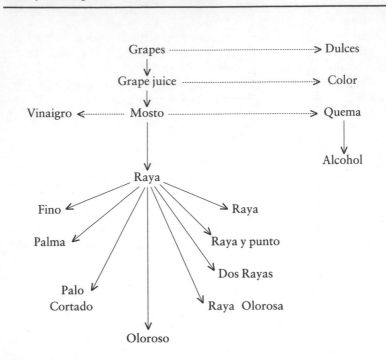

that the dead yeast cells at the bottom of the cask slowly autolyse, producing aldehydes. These may account for the typical fino 'twang', which you may find in this tasting. It is a 'compare and contrast' tasting, with the same grape (Palomino), the same reductive production technique, but a different vineyard and cellar ambience.

DRY FINO SHERRY/DRY (FINO) MONTILLA

The wines of Montilla-Moriles have many affinities with sherries, being made in similar ways, but using the Pedro Ximénez grapes, which in Jerez are employed principally for the fuller and richer styles. Hence, if you can get a sample of dry fino Montilla to compare with and contrast against the dry fino sherry, you can

Figure 11
Sherry development – finos, cortados and amontillados

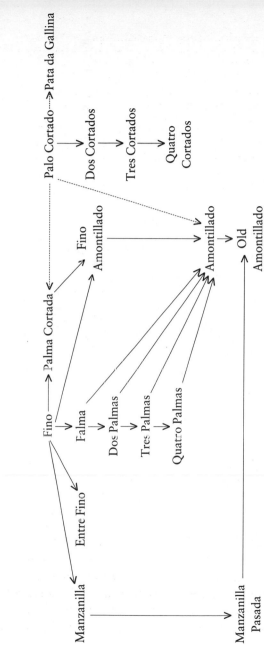

Figure 12
Sherry development – olorosos and rayas

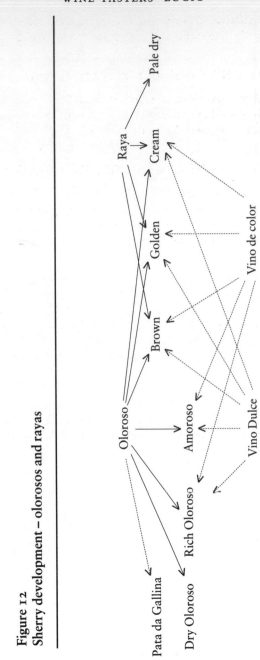

look for reductive similarities, against grape-variety differences, while making allowances for differences in ambience.

OLOROSO SHERRY/MONTILLA OLOROSO

If you can find a dry oloroso from Montilla-Moriles to taste against your dry oloroso sherry sample, you may be able to compare the oxidation effect on two different varieties.

DRY FINO MONTILLA/MONTILLA OLOROSO

Comparing two different Montilla styles may help to reinforce a sensory memory of the Pedro Ximénez variety, with a re-tasting of the fino and oloroso sherries to reinforce any distinctions from Palomino wines, and between reductive and oxidative effects.

OTHER STYLES – PALO CORTADO, DRY AMONTILLADO

The world of fine sherries has many subtleties, and it is not difficult to get hooked on them. You might then wish to try tasting palo cortado against dry amontillado, and each of them against finos and olorosos, in order to try to identify whether an amontillado may have started out in a reductive state, and then filled out and become nutty with oxidation, or whether it had originated as a palo cortado, or whether it might be a blended wine, from more than one origin, to achieve the typical amontillado style.

23

Deliberate Oxidation: Madeiras

THE MAKING OF MADEIRAS

The volcanic soil of Madeira produces wines with great keeping potential, and in the early days it was found that sending the wines in cask on long sea voyages – to the East and West Indies – helped to soften and improve them. Equatorial heat caused evaporation, ullages in the casks encouraged oxidation, and the long transits and the ship's movement matured and stabilized the wine. But it was expensive, and was replaced by the *estufa* procedure, by which the wines, in casks or vats, are heated to between 40 and 50°C, for a minimum of three months. After slow cooling, they are fortified up to 17 degrees of alcohol by volume for further maturation. (Some Madeiras are still made *without* being *estufado,* and are called *Canteiros.*)

The style of Madeiras, made with what is deliberate oxidation, is so distinctive that a table wine that has over-oxidized is said to be 'maderized'. What might be a defect in that table wine is a characteristic of Madeiras. So it may be useful to reinforce any oxidation/reduction lessons learnt with sherries, with the oxidation/baked character of Madeira. It may also help to identify the 'roasted' or 'baked' notes sometimes found in table wines and ports as a result of very hot summer temperatures causing thickening of the grape-skins.

As an example of a different effect of oxidation, Rosemary George draws attention to the unusual characteristics of white Côtes du Jura, which she describes as having a distinctive firm nuttiness.

TYPES OF MADEIRAS

The principal noble white grape varieties grown on the Island of Madeira gave their names to the main styles of wines produced and marketed: dry Sercial, medium-dry Verdelho, medium-rich Bual (or Boal), and rich sweet Malmsey (Malvasia). But the most widely planted grape (some 50 to 60 per cent of the total production), the Tinta Negra Mole, is a black-skinned grape, with greenish pulp, and is the one you are most likely to meet in any Madeira, which is only distinguished by an indication of its dryness or sweetness. Other noble grape varieties – Terrantez and Bastardo – are rarities. The Bastardo grape can produce a unique and distinctive aroma, as I discovered when I reintroduced its wines into the UK from Portugal after an absence of 250 years. I had been spurred to do so by the Shakespearean quotation: '. . . we shall have all the world drink brown and white bastard.'

MADEIRA STYLES

If you taste a Sercial against a Bual, you should look at them in a number of ways. Firstly you can note the difference in sweetness: Sercial is normally dry to extra-dry, with 0.5 to 1.5 degrees Baumé of residual sugar (see Tables 5 and 6, pp. 120 and 121); Bual is traditionally medium-sweet, with 2.5 to 3.5 degrees Baumé. Next you might try to assess any differences in acidity. Bual grows above 200 metres, whereas Sercial is grown higher up, about 700 metres above sea level. Sercial was believed to have affinities with Rhein-riesling, and, like its German counterpart, can produce quality in cooler conditions, with crisp acidity needing time to mature. Bual can mature faster, with milder characteristics.

SHERRIES VERSUS MADEIRAS

Like sherry, Madeira can be served as an aperitif, and with the soup course, as well as at other times. So you might try tasting fino sherry against Sercial, comparing similarities of weight, against differences of attack and finish, and whether the *estufado* character is detectable on the nose.

A tasting of fuller oxidation styles could compare and contrast

Table 5
Measurements of density

This table is an approximation based on French and German tables, using different instruments:

Specific Gravity	Degrees Oechsle	Degrees Brix	Degrees Baumé
1.000	0	0.00	0.00
1.005	5	1.25	0.71
1.010	10	2.50	1.43
1.015	15	3.75	2.12
1.020	20	5.00	2.75
1.025	25	6.25	3.43
1.030	30	7.50	4.14
1.035	35	8.75	4.86
1.040	40	10.00	5.71
1.042	42	10.50	6.00
1.045	45	11.00	6.11
1.049	49	12.20	7.00
1.053	53	13.00	7.22
1.057	57	14.00	7.77
1.061	61	15.00	8.32
1.063	63	15.70	9.00
1.070	70	17.50	10.00

Table 6
Measurements of sugar content

The presence of non-sugars in grape must means that sugar measurements made by specific gravity or refractometer need to be adjusted:

Specific gravity	Degrees Oechsle	Sugar content from Brix tables (grams/litre)	Adjusted sugar content (grams/litre)
1.060	60	155.7	130.3
1.070	70	181.9	156.7
1.080	80	208.1	183.1
1.090	90	234.2	209.5
1.100	100	260.6	235.9
1.110	110	286.8	262.3

oloroso sherry against Bual, noting differences of residual sugar, or concentration of extract, and length of finish.

Finally, this could be an exercise in imaginative tasting, thinking of all the different kinds of soup, from consommé to thick potage, and which wine (if any) would go best with each one.

TRANSMOGRIFICATION

Sercial has been likened to the German Riesling, so if any Sercial is left over from these tastings, it might be worth keeping it to compare with the Rheingau Riesling, which will be used in tastings in a later section. You can then judge for yourself whether the wines have any sensory affinities, apart from the fact that they both grow fairly high up the hills. And you can try to see if any sea-change from more northerly latitudes to more southerly climes might have changed the nature of the grape, apart from the differences in vinification.

RED TRANSMOGRIFICATIONS

Over the centuries, travellers have carried vine-cuttings from country to country. French vines may have been carried into Galicia by pilgrims going to Santiago di Compostella. The Syrah grape is reputed to have been brought from its native Syria to the Rhône Valley by a returning Crusader, to be planted on the hillside where he established his Hermitage. We are even told his name – the Chevalier de Stérimbourg. The Syrah is a noble grape, and is to be found, as well as its progenies, in many parts of the world.

Cape Hermitage, which I had mistakenly believed to be the Syrah variety, was in fact a Cinsault (spelt Cinsaut in South Africa), and it gave rise (in 1926) to a distinctive South African vine variety – Pinotage – a crossing of the Pinot Noir with the South African 'Hermitage' (i.e. Cinsault) vine. So a compare-and-contrast tasting of good Pinotage against a similarly priced Cinsault wine and a reliable Pinot Noir could be instructive.

The Australians have taken the Shiraz variety to their hearts, producing wines ranging from the eminently drinkable, through the robust, to fine keepable vintages. One might even be able to find a Californian Shiraz, in order to double-check whether the southern hemisphere effect could be stronger than the sea-change, or any effect of '*terroir*'.

The hemispheres do not come into the next exploration of vine-transportation. That distinctive Californian variety – Zinfandel – is thought to have originated from the Primitivo vine of southern Italy. Now that soundly made Primitivo wines are more readily available on the market, we may be able to put Primitivo/Zinfandel to the tasting test. It will be important to make sure that the Californian Zinfandel is a dry red wine, since wine-makers produce a range of styles, including sweet reds, light dry reds, and blush wines.

Chile produces many good table wines with varietal names well known from French origins – Chardonnay, Merlot, Cabernet Sauvignon. What may not be so well known is that the original plantings were made in the nineteenth century with cuttings from French pre-phylloxera vines. So we may be looking at a double-transformation (or even a triple one): French vines might have changed since phylloxera; we have the phase-reversal of the seasons in the southern hemisphere; and the climate patterns may well be different, since Chile is influenced by the cold Humboldt current, while France is more likely to feel some effect from the warm Gulf Stream. Hence it might be wise to keep an open mind when tasting Chilean varietals against European equivalents.

COLOUR CLONES

Most textbooks about the Rhône vineyards will mention the thirteen varieties that went to make the classic Châteauneuf-du-Pape, even though no more than nine vine types will normally be found in the vineyards. But the number of grape types could in practice have been more than thirteen, since some of the varieties, such as Grenache, can have white clones as well as the more usual red, and also a rosé version, known as Grenache Gris. A rosé wine, made from this pink Grenache, rejoices in the name 'Gris de Gris'.

The white Chasselas, which you find in Pouilly-sur-Loire wine (but *not* in Pouilly Fumé, which is made from Sauvignon Blanc grapes), has a pink version, the Chasselas Rose, more usually grown as an early table grape. The Pinot has gone through even more avatars – Pinot Blanc, Pinot Gris, Pinot Meunier, Pinot Noir – while in the Côte-d'Or the Pinot Noir fin is again subdivided into Pinot Noirien, Pinot Liebaud, and Pinot Beurot. And there is also the upright version of the Pinot Noir, the more prolific 'plant droit'.

It can all be rather confusing, since the more detailed one's studies of wine districts become, the more minor variations one comes across. When I was shipping Italian wines from the Novara hills, I was shown the local Nebbiolo vines, known as Spanna, and others, which were pointed out as Nebbiolo Barolo. But afterwards when I went to buy Barolo wines, the growers there subdivided their Barolo vines into Lampio, Michet and Rose'. So the opportunities for tuning and testing one's palate (and memory) can provide a life-time's challenge.

24

Different Acidities

MALIC AND TARTARIC ACIDS

It can be helpful if one can start to distinguish the 'green-apple' notes of malic acidity from the less 'mouth-puckering' but fuller acidity of tartaric, often found in wine as tartrates (see Fig. 15, p. 148). You look first for clues on the nose, and then on the palate.

DRY MOSELLE/DRY GRAVES

It is a truism that vineyards nearer the North Pole and South Pole are cooler than vineyards that are closer to the equator, and similarly, vineyards higher up a mountain tend to be cooler than those lower down. Malic acidity can break down in the grape under the influence of warmth and humidity, hence more malic acidity may be expected in wines from northerly and higher vineyards, such as the Moselle, when compared with the Graves district of Bordeaux, which is within a hundred metres or so of sea level, and under the tempering influence of the Atlantic.

If you taste a dry Moselle against a dry Graves, you should first take into account a difference in alcoholic strength: Moselles are low in alcohol (7 to 9 per cent of alcohol by volume (abv)), whereas Graves are usually 12 to 12.5 per cent abv. Higher alcohol can make a wine taste drier, and so can higher acidity – but in a different way. If you are thinking in terms of wine shapes, you might find that acidity thins a wine upwards, while alcohol dries a wine sideways, making it a bit broader.

On the nose, you should remember that the Moselle is most

probably from the Moselriesling variety, whereas the dry Graves could be predominantly (if not totally) Sauvignon Blanc. Some people suggest gooseberry notes as a clue to Sauvignon Blanc, but on other soils, such as the Tracy end of the Pouilly-sur-Loire district (where the grape variety is known as Blanc Fumé), you may find a suggestion of asparagus flavour.

DRY RHEINGAU RIESLING/DRY AUSTRALIAN RIESLING

Here you are likely to be tasting two wines from the same variety (Rheinriesling). Few growers would consider it worth their while to plant the Italic Riesling, which the Germans call Welschriesling, and which is labelled Laski Rizling in Former Yugoslavia.

Australian wine-growing conditions are less variable and less extreme than the Rhineland, so you are likely to find more ripeness, some more alcohol, and less malic acidity in the Australian wine. Look at the labels to check the alcohol content: the German wine could be between 8 and 10 per cent abv, and the Australian between 11 and 12 per cent abv, so the alcohol difference is likely to be less than the Moselle/Graves comparison. It may still be detectable, so it is worth looking for. But most of all, study the nose, and then the palate, and see if you think there may be a 'southerly' style of wine, distinguishable from a 'northerly' style of Rhine-wine.

ACETIC ACID

Left to itself, grape juice could ferment to alcohol, and then degrade to vinegar. These are the chemical formulae concerned:

$$C_6H_{12}O_6 => 2C_2H_6O + 2CO_2 + 23.5 \text{ cals}$$

Grape sugar yields ethyl alcohol plus carbon dioxide plus heat

This is called the Primary Fermentation, and is carried out by the enzyme *zymase*, produced by yeasts (usually *Saccharomyces ellipsoideus*). As a rule of thumb, one can reckon that each 18 grams of sugar per litre of juice has a potential of producing 1 per cent of alcohol; hence grape must with 216 grams of sugar per litre (approximately 12° Baumé) would be needed for a dry wine with 12 per cent of alcohol by volume (abv).

If oxidation occurs unchecked, acetic acid can be produced:

$$CH_3 CH_2 OH + O_2 => CH_3 COOH + H_2O$$

Alcohol plus oxygen gives acetic acid plus water

This imparts vinegar tastes to the wine, and 'volatile acidity' aromas, which the French refer to as *acéscence*, and which they differentiate from the typical vinegar smell.

DISCOVERING VOLATILITY

One of the difficulties that I found when trying to teach students about faulty wines was obtaining good samples of bad wines. Wines are seldom, if ever, static, and as soon as a wine develops one fault, other defects or changes are apt to come crowding on its heels. I would hope that none of the wines that you normally buy are faulty, so you may wish to try some 'do-it-yourself' volatility.

Get hold of a bottle of sound but inexpensive dry white table wine, and an empty clean half-bottle, and a stopper cork or taper cork. Alternatively, you may prefer two half-bottles of the wine, and an empty 75 cl. bottle. Also obtain a small quantity of white wine vinegar, and some cotton wool.

One half-bottle of the wine will be kept well corked as a 'control', so that you can eventually taste it against any 'volatile acidity' that you may be able to create in the rest of the wine. Pour a small amount of the white wine vinegar into the rest of the wine, shake it well (to introduce oxygen), smell it and taste it, so that you know what you started with, pour it into the 75 cl. bottle so that it is on ullage with an air space above the wine, and stopper the bottle with clean cotton wool.

With any luck, the addition of the vinegar will unbalance the wine, and start off an acetic fermentation, so that you are producing your own home-made wine vinegar. Smell and taste it every few days, to see what is happening, and when you think that you can detect volatile acidity on the nose, compare it with the original wine vinegar, and the original wine. You might find that the volatile acidity is producing higher notes on the aromas.

25

Acidity/Sweetness Balance

SWEETENING PROCEDURES

German wines are produced near the northern limit of the vine, and special skills and procedures have needed to be evolved to make balanced and drinkable wines in the less good years. One of these is the use of *Süssreserve*, sterile grape juice added to the wine *after* fermentation has finished. This should be contrasted with the procedure called *chaptalization* (named after Monsieur Jean Antoine Chaptal, 1756–1832) whereby dry cane sugar is added to the must *before* fermentation; the object of chaptalization is to raise the alcohol content of the ensuing wine, rather than to sweeten a dry wine. In Germany wet-sugaring has been permitted, since the water used to dissolve the sugar may help to reduce slightly the highish acidities of the less good years. In recent years, efforts have been made to promote the use of rectified grape juice instead of cane sugar as the sweetening agent, to help reduce the pressure on markets of overproduction of lower-grade wines (the so-called 'wine lake').

TASTING EXPERIMENTS

One way of learning more about acidity/sweetness balances in white wines is to add sugar to dry wines of different acidities, and then to see the effect of raising their acidities. One can, of course, add teaspoonfuls of sugar to glasses of wine, and stir, but household teaspoons vary in size, and so do glasses. For tasting experiments, extreme accuracy may not be necessary, which is just as well, since the relationship of sucrose, glucose and water seems rather complicated. Textbooks will tell you that a saturated solution of sucrose gives 67.1 per cent of solids at 20°C, and a supersaturated solution can contain up to 74 per cent of solids, but may behave differently in the presence of glucose.

For the purposes of our experiments, the easiest way of making a standard syrup is two cups of granulated sugar to one cup of water, heated to dissolve the sugar, boiled briefly, and then cooled. This is the kind of syrup (but with a teaspoonful of lemon juice added to invert the sucrose) that is used to pour over Turkish pastries after they have been baked. This should give a solution somewhere between 61° and 62° Brix, with a Specific Gravity at 20°C of approximately 1.300.

Most (if not all) of the tartaric content of wines is in the form of potassium hydrogen tartrate (potassium bitartrate) (see Table 2, p. 61), which in kitchen use is known as cream of tartar. Adding some of this to your wine may be the easiest way of raising acidity experimentally, although it may not dissolve very easily, without some stirring or shaking.

ACIDIFYING THE SAMPLES

Adding tartrate to the dry Moselle may make the wine drier, though maybe somewhat fuller. If this is so, try tasting it against your sample of dry Rheingau Riesling. If you find the treated sample fuller than the original Moselle, but less full than the Rheingau wine, you may get an idea what people mean when they say that the wines of the Nahe valley are between Moselle and Rheingau in style.

Now acidify similarly the Rheingau wine, and taste it against the Graves. This in turn can be acidified, and tasted. With the tastings of the natural and the treated examples of the three wines, you should try to fix in your perceptions and in your mind any differences in the way in which the two acids behave.

From a historical point of view, waterworks on the River Moselle have raised the water level, and the increased volume of water has influenced the microclimate, so present-day Moselle wines seem to have lower acidities than wines of the past. For maximum lightness and crisp acidities you might like to try wines from the Saar and Ruwer, the smaller tributaries of the Moselle.

SWEETENING THE SAMPLES

Adding sugar (or your sugar syrup) to the various wines, before and after the addition of tartrates, may provide enlightenment about the way that sweetness can mask acidity, and vice versa. After all, if you are eating stewed fruit and you find it too sour, you often add some more sugar.

The other thing that you should look for is whether there may be a point when excessive sweetening makes a wine lose character, and become bland, or flabby. If you are tasting with other people, you may well find differences of opinion. Some folk may be relatively sugar-intolerant, and others acid-intolerant. You need to know where you yourself stand.

SPARKLING WINE BALANCES

At this point it might be helpful to consider acidity/sweetness balances in sparkling wines. After disgorging, it is the rare *extra-brut* sparkling wine that does not have a *dosage* of sweetening; most sparkling wines have quite a high acidity, and if they are not of very high quality they usually need a *dosage* to round off the rough edges. The high-quality wines of nil or low *dosage* will need time to fill out and round off.

If you start off by tasting inexpensive wines made by the *cuve close* (Charmat closed vat) procedure, and taste their *brut* against their medium-dry style, you will probably be tasting wines of a similar price, and made from the same type of basic wine – the only difference being the *dosage*. You may then move on to try similar tasting with pairs of wines from other wine-growing regions and countries, and try to assess whether there may be a quality or style difference as well as a sweetness difference.

Some people believe that the carbon dioxide gas content of a sparkling wine can affect the apparent dryness of a wine; that (they say) is why the more acid wines of a region are usually made into sparkling wine. One way of testing this theory is by putting a still white wine sample through a soda-making machine, and tasting the result against an untreated control sample. But be warned: wine does not behave the same as water in a carbonating machine, and is apt to bubble over when you press the knob; care and caution are needed to avoid an extensive mopping-up operation.

26

Three-Way Balance

ALCOHOL/ACIDITY BALANCE IN WHITE WINES

The three wines in our experiments – Moselle, Rheingau and Graves – were (we presume) reasonably balanced dry wines; in other words, they did not rely on residual sugars, but on the original balance between alcohol and acidity. If we are now going to experiment with the effect of alcohol on the balance of white wines, we need to have a neutral alcohol that we can add to them, and see the effect on nose and taste. Since pharmacists do not hand over potable alcohol on request, a neutral vodka (or *wódka*) would seem to be the simplest additive. An alternative might be Polish High strength Pure Spirit, but this will require recalculation of the amounts needed.

As a control, re-taste the original wines, add extra spirit, and taste the result to learn the effect of the alcohol on the two-way alcohol/acidity balance. You can then add alcohol to the acidified samples, to learn the effect of alcohol *and* acidity on the balance.

ALCOHOL/ACIDITY/SWEETNESS BALANCES

Having explored the effect of two-way balances in white wines, you can now make a start on three-way balances. Take the three samples to which you have already added sugar syrup (as suggested above), add alcohol to them, and taste against the original controls. Then do the same with the samples that have additional acidity and sweetness.

If you think back over this series of tastings, you may well have learnt quite a lot about wine styles and balances. But you may also have gleaned something about your own personal tastes, and what your tolerances may be for alcohol, acidity and sweetness. And if you have been tasting in a group, you may well have discovered something about other people's tastes. A group tasting may also have impressed on you the difficulty of 'sticking to your guns' and holding on to original perceptions and impressions, in the face of peer pressure, or the expert opinions of a 'guru' who may have helped you to organize these tastings. Nobody except you can possibly know what goes on inside your own nose and mouth!

27
Tannin Characteristics

INTERNATIONAL STANDARDS

The International Standards on Sensory Analysis cover three main fields: Methodology (i.e. how to set up tastings to obtain reproducible results); Vocabulary (defining the tasting terms in French and English, which are two of the three official ISO languages – the other being Russian); and Training.

In the ISO Vocabulary, the persimmon, or kaki fruit, with its mouth-puckering tannins, is used to define the term 'bitter', so if you can get hold of an original persimmon, it might be as well to taste it. This is not the same as the more widely available 'Sharon fruit' from Israel, which is a highly developed variety with much less of the original tannins. When fully ripe, a persimmon should have a semi-translucent skin.

TANNIN POWDER

In the past, when we fined white wines in order to clarify them, using gelatine fining powder, it was recommended that we should add some tannin and rouse it well into the cask before starting to add the finings, which we whisked into some of the wine, and then poured into the cask and stirred around with a broom handle. I know that the textbooks showed pictures of rousing-rods with long whiskers, but we never bothered with such niceties. The idea of using the tannin powder was that the fining would act on it, and not remove flavour tannins from the wine.

GALLO-TANNINS

The casks in which wines are stored and matured can impart distinctive tannin notes to the wine, and can play a significant part in its future evolution and development. As recently as thirty to fifty years ago, there were marked differences in the ways that growers used casks. I found it interesting to note the different way that casks were regarded in Bordeaux and Burgundy.

It was generally accepted that top claret châteaux (who could afford the outlays) used new oak casks for all their best new wines. By way of contrast, top burgundy wines were put into casks of *troisième envinage* – three-year-old casks. In Burgundy, new casks were used for *vin ordinaire*, which might benefit from a bit of stiffening-up. The next year the casks were used for *village* wines (ordinary Gevrey-Chambertin, Nuits-St-Georges or Beaune, for example), and only in their third year would a *Grand Vin* be put into them. This difference of approach reinforced my theory that red Bordeaux traditionally depended on extract for its body, whereas burgundy relied more on alcohol for its weight.

OAK VERSUS CHESTNUT

Oak casks were expensive, and maturing casks could be made with relatively thin staves, compared with transport casks, which needed thicker staves to resist the buffeting they received as they travelled back and forth; so transport casks were usually made of more neutral chestnut wood.

There was a difference in the Beaujolais/Mâconnais region, where the red wines were largely made from the Gamay grape *(Gamay rouge à jus blanc)*. The Gamay wine, when stored in oak, can produce coffee notes on the nose, so the red wines of Beaujolais were normally stored in chestnut casks, or vats.

In North America, another cask-wood dimension may come into play, since wine-makers may well have been using redwood for the larger casks and vats.

OAKED STYLES

You can sometimes come across wine-growers who produce oaked and unoaked versions of the same (or similar) white wine. If you can find them, you should seize the opportunity to explore how oak can affect the aroma, flavour, and development of wines. A pair of wines of a recent vintage may reveal vanilla notes on the nose from the oaking; and some people might prefer the stronger primary notes (flower and/or fruit, soil character, freshness) of the unoaked style, which may be covered or masked by the oak-notes on nose and palate. This may explain why some wines are criticized for being 'over-oaked'.

If you can get a pair of older wines, with similar origin but one of them oaked and the other unoaked, you can then try to find out how oak can alter the evolution of a wine. You might find that the oak brings forward the complexing of the nose, and the appearance of secondary aromas. You can then decide for yourself whether (at least in the case of the wines you are studying) the effect of oak has hastened or slowed-down maturity on the palate. Finally, as an exercise in imaginative tasting, make a guess which of the two might be the longer-lasting and/or more interesting in the long run.

TASTING FOR TANNINS

Just as we had earlier tried to find ways of discovering a taster's likes and dislikes, acuities and tolerances, in relation to acidity and sweetness, so it might be helpful to try to do the same with regard to tannins. Before embarking on a voyage through the world of red wines, it might be salutary to have a look at teas, and their tannins. You may already know what you like – Indian tea or China tea – and what would be your choice in different situations. A person might choose a lighter, more fragrant tea for refreshment on a hot summer's day, and a stronger, more concentrated cup as a pick-me-up when tired on a cold winter's evening. The Chinese serve a relatively light tea throughout the meal to accompany the food, and then offer tiny cups of a very concentrated tea at the end as a digestive.

If you have a selection of teas available, taste them (rather than just drinking them), and try to see them in wine terms: aroma, balance, extract, quality. Remember that Earl Grey tea has added oil of bergamot, so it should be considered like a flavoured wine. Lapsang Souchong, which has been laid on tarred ropes, should be reserved for a time when you are studying the wines of Barolo; some of the barolo soils impart a *catrame* (tarry) character to the Nebbiolo grapes.

Next you should remember that black teas are withered, rolled and fermented before being fired, whereas green teas are steamed to prevent fermentation, before rolling and firing. The fermentation may convert some of the tannins into sugars, so that Chinese green teas can contain nearly 40 per cent more tannins that similar Chinese black teas, which are sometimes referred to as red teas.

THE 'TEA-TASTER'S GUIDE TO WINE'

Some years ago, I was asked to write articles for the colour supplement of *The Observer*; trying to 'de-mystique' wines, I suggested that a person's taste for tea might suggest their taste for wines. If you want to try it out, see the suggested schedule of strong, medium and weak brews of Indian teas and China teas, alone, with lemon, with lemon and sugar, with milk, and with milk and sugar (see Figure 13).

At the end of the article, I suggested that weak China tea with lemon and sugar might indicate a Moselle-drinker, that medium black tea or China tea without sugar or milk might point to a preference for claret, and that if your tastes ran to 'sergeant-major's tea' – strongly brewed black tea with sweetened condensed milk – you might be happiest with fortified British Ruby wine.

THE ROLE OF THE ROSÉ

Rosé wines are apt to receive a bad press from serious wine buffs. Before the days of social correctness, they were apt to be dismissed as 'ladies' wines'. Now, even worse, they may simply be dismissed. Which is a pity, because the bad old days, when a restaurant 'carafe rosé' was produced by mixing red wines and white wines, are long past; as is the association of 'pink champagne' with Montmartre of the naughty nineties.

Figure 13
Wine-taster's 'tea-tasting' schedule

	Alone	With lemon	Lemon and sugar	With milk	Milk and sugar
Weak China tea					
Medium China tea					
Strong China tea					
Weak Indian tea					
Medium Indian tea					
Strong Indian tea					

The Loire Valley has a long tradition of eminently drinkable to excellent rosé and light red wines. The serious taster may want to take advantage of them to introduce colour tannins on to his palette. The two main red grapes of the region are the Gros-lot (or Grolleau), used to make the lower-priced Anjou rosés, and the Cabernet Franc, which can produce rosé wines with character, and makes the fine Loire red wines of Chinon, Bourgueil and Saint-Nicholas-de-Bourgueil.

If you want to taste a Rosé d'Anjou against a Cabernet Rosé, in order to try to distinguish any differences between the grape varieties, you may need to make allowances, as the *appellation* regulations were changed some time ago, making Cabernet d'Anjou a dry style of wine, against the off-dry to medium style of the Rosé d'Anjou.

Since we are now studying the effects of tannin, let us then go on to compare a good Cabernet Rosé against a Chinon Rouge, which is a light red wine that can take a certain amount of bottle-age. Before the Second World War, some French perfumers used to make a scent entitled '*foin coupé*' – new-mown hay – and this is the characteristic that I look for on the nose when approaching a Cabernet Franc wine. Some people use the term 'grassy', and the Italians use the word '*erbace*'.

SENSATIONS, TEXTURES AND SHAPES

But as this is a chapter about tannins, we should particularly look at any similarities and differences on the palate, and in the mouth. It could be helpful to organize our thinking in terms of sensations, textures, and shapes.

Earlier in this study, I had suggested that some people recognize tannins as a sensation of roughness or furriness on the inside of their cheeks. One might assume that the rosé had only been in contact with the skins for (say) twenty-four hours, whereas the red wine was probably macerated for several days, or even a week or two. So we should start by seeing if we find different sensations of roughness or furriness in the mouth, when tasting the rosé and the red wine. If we do, we are probably looking at a quantitative difference in the tannin content, due to the different length of time in contact with the skins. Can we now, by chewing the wines and mixing them with saliva, find a difference in the time it takes for the tannins to produce a grittiness when we rub the tongue against the roof of the mouth? And if there is such a difference, could we then use it as a scale to measure tannin?

Next, let us move on to the subject of texture. People often use the phrase 'a rough red wine'; would you put Chinon Rouge into that category? And which is rougher or smoother – the red or the rosé?

Finally, how about the Gestalt psychology concept of shapes and forms? Which is the lighter or heavier? Which is the deeper in flavour? And is one longer than the other, with flavours lingering on the palate?

I personally have a great liking for many of the fine Loire wines, so I would be tempted to round off this tasting by introducing a red Bourgueil or, better still, a Saint-Nicholas-de-Bourgueil, and tasting it against the Chinon. The soils are different, although the grape is nearly always the same Cabernet Franc, and I think that the textures come out quite differently, with a mature Chinon shining with satin elegance, and the mature Bourgueil more silkily velvety.

28

Four-Way Balance

SWEETNESS IN RED WINES

When we start tasting sweet red wines, we are adding another dimension (residual sugar) to our previous approach to dry red wines. Alternatively, we are adding another dimension (tannins) to the way we were tasting sweet white wines. Since highly tannic white wines are fortunately rare, we are perforce looking at sweet red wines to find examples of four-way balance.

In tasting experiments on white wines we had suggested adding sugar syrup to dry wine, so we might try the same approach, and add some of our syrup to a dry red wine. A second tasting experiment could add sweetness plus extra alcohol.

Some of the late-Victorian or Edwardian wine writers make mention of 'ported clarets'. This probably reflects the desperate measures that were required in the dire days following phylloxera, when the vineyards had been devastated, and the replanted vines were not yet producing the required quality. So an addition of fortified sweet red wine to the sample of dry red wine could be another way of checking our tasting abilities with four-way assessment. The fortified red wine will be adding tannins and acids, as well as extract, to the dry red wine, so this second 'tweaked' sample should be tasted against the one that was simply sweetened with sugar syrup, and the one with sugar and alcohol added, in order to note the differences in balance. At the end of such a series of tastings, it might be possible to get an inkling of the relative effects of the various wine components on that elusive concept of 'body'.

MULLED WINE

Making a good mulled wine is really a hands-on exercise in creative three-way or four-way balance. Adding citrus (oranges and lemons) to a cheap and cheerful dry red wine raises the acidity, as well as introducing fruit sugars, which usually do not fully counter the drying effects of the acidity and the spices. So you generally need to add some sugar, white sugar for a neutral effect, or brown sugar for different flavour and a bit more extract. Heating seems to make the wine's alcohol more heady, but some people like to boost the strength with an addition of brandy; this will tend to make the mixture a bit drier again, and reduce the fruit flavours.

For people who do not like their mulled wine too sweet, one way round is to boost the 'fruit' notes. Here you could take a tip from the old Burgundian *fraudeurs*, who used locally grown and made cassis to improve their red wines after the phylloxera epidemic. For us, the easy way is to add a dash of blackcurrant juice, filched from the children's bottle of Ribena or similar.

29

Concentration of Extract

─────

DRY EXTRACT

When tasting a wine, the perceived 'body' of the wine may be influenced by a number of components, such as alcohol; quantity and type of acidity; residual sugars; and 'extract'. One may visualize the vine-roots 'extracting' nutrients from the soil, which are then transformed by the metabolism of the vine, and metamorphosed during vinification and maturing.

The classic analysis of wines may include measuring the 'dry extract' by evaporating a measured quantity of wine, to drive off the liquid components, and then weighing the dry residue. The extract may also be estimated from the specific gravity, using Tables 5 (p. 120), 6 (p. 121), 7 and 8 (pp. 143–4). For this, one needs to remember that increasing quantities of alcohol *lower* the density (specific gravity) of a mixture of alcohol and water (see Table 8), whereas sugars etc. *raise* the density (see Tables 5 and 6). The rule-of-thumb formula for this calculation of extract is as follows:

$$d_2 = (d + 1) - d_1$$

where
d_2 = specific gravity (SG) of extract (see Table 7)
d = specific gravity (SG) of the wine (see Table 5)
d_1 = specific gravity (SG) of the alcohol content (see Table 8)

With sweet wines one may wish to calculate the balance of extract, or 'extract without sugar', by subtracting the residual sugars in grams per litre from the total extract in grams per litre (see Table 6).

Table 7
Calculation of wine extract

Specific gravity at 15°c	Extract (grams/ litre)	Specific gravity at 15°c	Extract (grams/ litre)	Specific gravity at 15°c	Extract (grams/ litre)
1.0040	9.6	1.0105	25.2	1.0170	41.4
1.0045	10.8	1.0110	26.4	1.0175	42.9
1.0050	12.0	1.0115	27.6	1.0180	44.3
1.0055	13.2	1.0120	28.8	1.0185	45.8
1.0060	14.4	1.0125	30.0	1.0190	47.2
1.0065	15.6	1.0130	31.2	1.0195	48.7
1.0070	16.8	1.0135	32.4	1.0200	50.1
1.0075	18.0	1.0140	33.6	1.0205	51.6
1.0080	19.2	1.0145	34.8	1.0210	53.0
1.0085	20.4	1.0150	36.0	1.0215	54.4
1.0090	21.6	1.0155	37.2	1.0220	55.9
1.0095	22.8	1.0160	38.5	1.0225	57.3
1.0100	24.0	1.0165	40.0	1.0230	58.8

CONCENTRATION ON THE VINE

The amount of minerals and other nutrients that the vine-plant will extract from the vineyard soil and lodge in the grapes varies, owing to a number of factors. Some soils are richer or more mineralized than others. Rootstocks can behave differently. Some rootstocks of riparian ancestry spread shallowly but widely, originally influenced by water-table and a sandy-silty soil structure. Others delve deep down into subsoil. If you visit the cellars of Château Ausone, you may see rootlets emerging from the cave-like cellar roof, belonging to vines in the vineyards metres above.

A young vine will have a less developed root system than an old-established vine; the older the vine, the more 'extract' you could expect. Pruning can govern the size of the plant, and influence its yields. Hence pruning can change the relationship of the vine's top-hamper, of branches, shoots, leaves and bunches, compared

Table 8
Measurement of alcohol in a mixture of alcohol and water

Alcoholic strength at 15°c	Grams of alcohol in 100g mixture (Percentage by weight)	Grams of alcohol per litre of mixture at 15°c	Density of mixture (SG) at 15°c
0	0.000	0.000	1.00000
1	0.795	7.936	0.99844
2	1.593	15.873	0.99695
3	2.394	23.809	0.99592
4	3.196	31.745	0.99413
5	4.001	39.682	0.99277
6	4.807	47.618	0.99145
7	5.616	55.554	0.99016
8	6.426	63.491	0.98891
9	7.238	71.427	0.98770
10	8.050	79.364	0.98652
11	8.867	87.300	0.98537
12	9.685	95.236	0.98424
13	10.503	103.175	0.98314
14	11.324	111.109	0.98206
15	12.146	119.045	0.98100
16	12.696	126.982	0.97995
17	13.794	134.918	0.97892
18	14.621	142.854	0.97790
19	15.499	150.791	0.97688
20	16.279	158.727	0.97587
21	17.111	166.663	0.97487
22	17.944	174.600	0.97387
23	18.779	182.736	0.97286
24	19.616	190.472	0.97185
25	20.455	198.409	0.97084
26	21.495	206.345	0.96981
27	22.138	214.281	0.96876
28	22.984	222.218	0.96769
29	23.832	230.154	0.96759
30	24.683	238.091	0.96545

with its root-development. Weather plays its part, with rain diluting juices, and sunshine heat concentrating them.

Vintage reports about the weather during the time that the grapes were developing may give the taster some clues as to what to expect, as will a mention on the label of *vieilles vignes* – you may expect more extract from the old vines. In a year when the weather threatens over-cropping, or uneven development of the bunches following an over-long flowering period, or rain dilution, the grower may proceed to a 'green harvest', and send workers through the vineyard during the summer, to thin out the crop, and discard the bunches that are unlikely to ripen properly. The Germans term this a *Vorlese*, and it favours the remaining crop with a better chance of quality.

DEGREES OF RIPENESS

From the vine's point of view, *physiological maturity* is reached when sufficient materials have assembled in the pips for them to be viable and to germinate when planted. From the vine-grower's point of view, *industrial maturity* is only reached when sufficient sugars have assembled in the juice for wine to be made from it. Although in some favoured vineyards the two kinds of maturity may coincide, in most of the cooler vineyards considerable time may elapse before economic harvesting can occur.

We must also remember that grapes grow in bunches, and that each vine will carry a number of bunches. One might consider that, ideally, all the vines' flower buds would open at the same time as bees and other insects are flying around to pollinate, so that all the grapes in all the bunches on all the vines would reach ripeness together. However, there would probably not be enough harvesters available to gather in such a bumper crop, and in reality this seldom if ever happens.

Some varieties of grape ripen earlier, and some later; free-draining soils warm up earlier, and heavy clay soils retain moisture and keep cooler, until they bake hard and heat up. Slopes that face the sun ripen the grapes quicker. So the wine-grower arranges sequential and/or selective harvesting. This can be seen most clearly in the vineyards of Germany and Austria, where you may find it enshrined in the wine laws, and recorded in the labelling. In order to avoid confusion of nomenclature, we shall restrict ourselves (for a start) to Germany.

The timing of the main harvest is largely governed by weather, but also by availability of pickers. So the grower may have to instruct the pickers to gather up bunches with some less mature grapes in them, to make standard wine in order to ensure his cash-flow. But if he can assemble enough bunches of ripe grapes to make wine without needing to improve it with added sweetening, he can opt for the first of the predicate wines – 'Kabinett', which is a *Qualitätswein mit Prädikat* (QmP).

Spätlese (or Spaetlese, which is the alternative spelling) means 'late-gathered'; so, by definition, the wine is made from grapes harvested some time after the main harvest. Also, by law, the grapes must be fully ripe. Since the term is added after the wine name, this is also a predicate wine (QmP). And because of the 'fully ripe' requirement, it is usually a sweeter wine than Kabinett. When you come across a dry *(trocken)* Spätlese, you may expect it to have more attack and body due to a higher alcohol content (Figure 14).

Auslese wines are a higher category of QmP wines than Spätlese, since the wine law requires them to have a higher specific gravity,

Figure 14
Degrees of ripeness

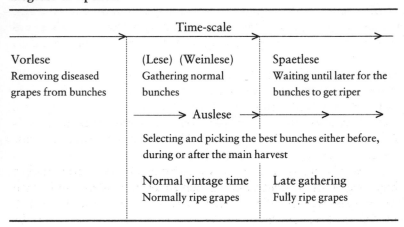

	Time-scale	
Vorlese Removing diseased grapes from bunches	(Lese) (Weinlese) Gathering normal bunches	Spaetlese Waiting until later for the bunches to get riper
	Auslese →	→ →
	Selecting and picking the best bunches either before, during or after the main harvest	
	Normal vintage time Normally ripe grapes	Late gathering Fully ripe grapes

expressed in degrees Oechsle (see Table 5, p. 120). But their quality does not necessarily come from a later stage in time-evolution than Spätlese, because Auslese means 'selection'. Skilled pickers are needed for Auslesen, either to pick only fully ripe bunches from the vine, or to pick only the ripe grapes and leave others to ripen further, or to weed out faulty or unripe grapes from otherwise ripe bunches. Hence, in a vintage when the flowering has been prolonged, when fully ripe grapes may be available interspersed among just-ripe grapes, a grower might send his team of skilled pickers through the vineyard to pick for his vats of Auslese, while unskilled pickers follow them through the rows of vines picking the rest of the grapes for ordinary QbA (*Qualitätswein bestimmter Anbaugebiete*) wines.

Once full maturity has been reached, all exchanges between the vine and the grape cease (even while the grape is still hanging on the vine). But developments continue *within* the grape. This is the period known as supermaturity (*surmaturation*). Malic acid decomposes more or less rapidly under the influence of temperature. The liquid part of the grape juice evaporates, influenced by temperature and humidity; higher temperatures hasten evaporation, but humidity may inhibit it. If the evaporation is faster than the decomposition of the malic acid, acidity may rise, especially if there is a fairly high tartaric content (see Figure 15). In either case, evaporation concentrates the sugar content. The skin of the grapes thins and becomes less resistant to cryptogamic infection. With suitable conditions, *Botrytis cinerea* – grey mould, can become 'noble. rot' (see p. 40), known in French as *pourriture noble*, and in German as *Edelfäule*; its mycelia penetrate the grape-skins, and help the evaporation and partial desiccation. The micro-organisms take nourishment from the grape juice, but feed more on the organic acids than on the sugars, so that they ameliorate the sugar/acid balance, and produce natural glycerine in the grape juice. They can also impart the characteristic 'noble' aroma. This is difficult to describe, but is something like, but nicer than, the ripe smell of a 'sleepy' and overripe pear.

A special quality of Auslese wine, from selected berries with a high degree of concentration, is named Beerenauslese; and when the grapes are shrivelled to almost-raisin concentration, it will be Trockenbeerenauslese. On the time-scale, these will usually be

Figure 15
Acidity Data

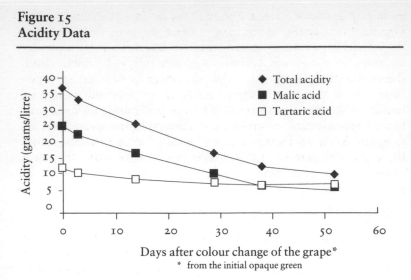

Days after colour change of the grape*
* from the initial opaque green

picked quite a while after the Spätlese harvest. However, in Germany you may see skilled pickers with sickle-shaped containers hung on the edges of their harvesting-tubs, into which they can separate the Auslese, Beerenauslese, and Trockenbeerenauslese grapes, while the ordinary bunches go into the tubs.

Grapes may be left even later on the vines, to await a hard frost; the frozen grapes must be gathered before the sun can warm them, and must immediately be pressed, with the ice crystals still inside them, as the juice will have been further concentrated by leaving the water behind in the form of ice in the winepress. This concentrated juice, made into Eiswein, has high acidity, special quality and character, and long-lasting potential. It can only be made from fully ripe grapes, since semi-ripe grapes, when caught by the frost, impart an unpleasantly acrid flavour, known in German as *Frostgeschmack*.

CONCENTRATION IN THE BUNCH

Techniques for concentrating the juices within the grapes, either on or off the vine, or sorting the grapes to make the wine only from selected high quality must, can be found in many forms and in widely varied wine regions. In the past in Spain, and still in Cyprus, for example, grapes are 'sunned' on mats to concentrate the juice. There is an old tradition in the Rhône Valley of a similar technique to make *Vin de Paille*. In Italy, you find *passito* wines, sometimes made by drying the bunches of grapes on racks in open sheds, while *recioto* wines were made selectively from the upper grapes of the bunches, since the 'shoulders' (*recie*) of the bunch were deemed to have received the maximum of overhead sunlight. In Spain, Moscatel Fino grapes are sunned for 10 to 12 days, and Pedro Ximénez are sunned for 18 to 20 days, to make the *vinos dulces* for sweet sherries.

CONCENTRATION FOR RED WINES

The wine-maker will have a problem with red grapes that lack concentration. If there has been a lot of rain, the juice is likely to have become dilute and watery, and prolonged *cuvaison* to produce an adequate colour will only yield thin tannic wines; the surface-to-volume ratio of skins to pulp (see p. 31) is out of balance. Conscientious wine-makers now tend to carry out a 'bleeding' (*saignée*) of the vat, drawing off a quantity of juice, so that the juice-to-skins proportion becomes more normal. The drawn-off juice can sometimes be made into a pleasant light rosé.

VALPOLICELLA/DRY AMARONE

One of the few comparative tastings of different concentrations of extract in red wines available to the general run of wine-tasters is with red wines from the Veneto region of northern Italy. In Valpolicella (as in some other places), they make a concentrated, long-lasting red wine from super-ripe grapes, which is called Amarone. Often, it is fermented as a rich sweet dessert wine, but dry Amarones do exist, which you could taste against a really good normal Valpolicella. You will need to make an allowance for difference in alcoholic content: the normal wine will probably have a strength of around 12.5 per cent abv, while the Amarone will be at least 14 per cent abv. The difference in concentration of 'fruit' and acidity will almost certainly be masked by the strength of the tannins.

Amarones are wines destined to take bottle-age; in Italy there was a tradition of keeping this kind of wine in bottle until it had thrown a deposit, and taken a tawny-orangey colour, and then serving it at the end of the meal as a dessert wine with fruit and nuts. Often, such wines need to 'breathe' and take up oxygen before the aroma opens up and shows its quality. You may sometimes hear Italians talking appreciatively about '*fund de buto*', the glass or two at the bottom of a bottle, saved as a treat for the next day's enjoyment, since it will have developed extra qualities from the additional breathing. I sometimes wonder whether the concentration of Amarones as young wines keeps them for a long time in a reductive state, so that they might need to oxidise more before they are enjoyed.

30
Practising Decanting

OPINIONS ABOUT DECANTING

Decanting was logical as well as aesthetic in the days when wines were stored and matured in a family's basement wine cellar. One might not want to bring dusty and cobwebby bottles into an elegant dining-room. Moreover, some wines, such as old vintage ports, had sealing-wax to protect the corks against cork-weevil, and chipping it away was a messy business. So the wine would be taken from its bin, rack or case, opened and decanted with a minimum of movement, and the brilliant wine taken upstairs in its decanter, with the branded cork held with two pins on a chain hanging round the decanter-neck.

With the change in drinking habits, and the making of eminently drinkable younger wines, and older wines with little or no deposit, decanting went out of fashion, aided no doubt by the vogue for specially designed bottles and elegant wine labels.

The practice of using a 'wine cradle' is no real substitute when the wine has a deposit; the first one or two glasses may come out star-bright when served from the cradle, but the repeated tilting and levelling as you go round the table filling glasses is almost certain to stir any deposit, so that the later servings are likely to be progressively unsatisfactory. The only sure way to use a cradle is to line up all the glasses side by side, with a few extra glasses at the end, and then to pour all the wine out in one continuous movement, until the last glass shows some deposit clouding.

LEARNING DECANTING

In the days when most champagne was disgorged *à la volée*, the disgorgers were highly skilled (and highly paid) employees. They were handling a high-value product, as were the *remueurs* who would shake the bottles and work them neck downwards on the *pupitres*; so untrained personnel could not be employed for these tasks. Trainees were therefore made to hone their skills on dummy bottles. Champagne bottles were filled with a supersaturated solution of rock salt, producing a deposit that behaved in many ways like the dead yeasts and tartrates. Trainee *remueurs* could work the dummy deposit down on to the corks, by progressively shaking and tilting the bottles, and other trainees could then practise flying the cork, together with the deposit, while losing the minimum of liquid.

DUMMY DECANTING

If we want to borrow the champagne ideas in order to learn, or hone, decanting skills, we need to get hold of rock salt. The kind of salt that is used for de-icing roads in winter-time will do well, as it contains enough impurities to create a convincing deposit in a bottle. Then assemble a number of clean and empty white Bordeaux bottles, similarly some empty claret and/or port bottles, and maybe some red burgundy bottles also. For the sake of simplicity, you will be using either stopper corks or taper corks, since either type is easy to put in or get out of the bottles; so you will need at least as many corks as you have bottles.

Now make a supersaturated solution of the rock salt by adding the salt to boiling water until no more will dissolve. Warm the bottles, so that they will not crack when the hot solution is poured into them. Stir the salt solution, so that the impurities are floating around, and fill it into half the number of each type of bottle, and put in the cork. You will keep the rest of the bottles empty, since you will want to decant into them. Lay the filled bottles down on their sides, and let them rest for whatever time is needed for the deposit to settle along the bottom side of the bottle. You can judge what is going on by looking at the transparent white bottles. You can assume that much the same will be happening in the green bottles.

DECANTING DRILL

When you and the dummies are ready for the first decanting practice, take some of the filled white bottles and stand them upright, an hour or so beforehand, so that the deposit starts to slide down the side of the bottle to collect on one side of the punt. Traditionally, decanting is done by candle-light, but a suitable electric torch is a reasonable alternative. Arrange the light source at a convenient height and position, so that it can be seen through the bottle that is being decanted. Holding the full bottle in one hand, with the deposit on the side nearest to the empty 'decanter' bottle, you start to pour gently and steadily. The decanter can either be standing on the table, or held in the other hand.

For the first part of the pouring operation, clear liquid should be flowing; then you may see a slight cloudy swirl arising from the deposit, and as the bottle approaches the horizontal, the deposit may start to move along the bottom side of the bottle, to reach the shoulder. I usually keep a spare glass on the decanting table, and when the swirl has reached the neck, I stop pouring into the decanter, and pour into the spare glass. Thus I can often get an extra glassful of wine, with only the slightest haze from the swirl, and keep the wine in the decanter star-bright. I can then decide whether I shall drink the hazy glassful myself, and leave all the decanter to my guests, or whether the haze has impaired the quality of the wine.

Having successfully completed your dummy decanting, you can pour the decanted liquid back into the original bottle, cork it again, shake well, and lay it down to rest for another practice session in a few days' time.

Once you have gained confidence with the white bottles, try it all again with the claret bottles, until you are sure you can see the swirls and deposit through the coloured glass. Then try again with the burgundy bottles, to discover the extent to which the more angular shoulders of the Bordeaux bottles help in decanting.

DECANTER VERSUS DREGS

Your acquired decanting skills can allow you to reprise your studies of tannins. For this, you need a bottle of mature red wine that has thrown a deposit. Decant this wine carefully, and pour the dregs into a glass. Cover the glass with a saucer, so that the dregs do not oxidize too much. Let the dregs settle for a quarter of an hour, and pour off the slightly cloudy top half into a clean glass, leaving the heavy deposit in the first glass.

Now carry out a comparative tasting of the three versions – decanted wine, light deposit, heavy dregs. This may give you a fresh insight into why we lay wines down to mature, what changes may be occurring during maturation, and why we may need to decant fine wines.

If you find differences in the aroma, you may wish to be reminded of the late Ronald Avery's championship of decanting; he believed that fine white burgundies (which would normally not have any deposit demanding decanting) greatly benefited from being decanted, since it opened up the bouquet and broadened the flavours.

31

Recording the Tastings

═══════

NOTEBOOKS

Michael Broadbent, in his book *Wine Tasting*, recommends the recording of tasting notes in pocket-sized notebooks, and describes the method he teaches and uses. The notebooks are opened sideways, so that the pages are used 'landscape', with columns for appearance, nose, taste, etc., which are ruled up in advance.

Michael has used them successfully for many years, and the small format encourages brevity. You record only whatever is significant, and tend to omit repetitive detail. It may demand a retentive memory for the fuller picture, which the brief notes may revive.

PRO-FORMA SHEETS

When I started tasting, I duplicated a number of blank tasting sheets, with headings to remind me of a tasting sequence, so that I would not miss anything out. At the top I put the country of origin of the wine (e.g. France), the wine region (e.g. Bordeaux) and the date of the tasting. This helped with the filing. Next headings were 'Where', 'When' and 'With whom'. This often helped me to recall in my mind's eye the occasion of the tasting, and bring back a lot of the details. It also helped to adjust the possibility of bias, since I had found that some people with whom I had tasted were very persuasive, and I might need to discount some of the eulogies that I had noted.

After a while I found that the files of these quarto-sized tasting-notes were proliferating and becoming unwieldy for easy reference, so I started another, parallel system.

CARD-INDEX RECORDS

Index cards were an everyday item of office use, so I prepared a card for each interesting wine that I tasted, or might want to discuss with clients. On the front I wrote, on the top line, the vintage (or NV for non-vintage), the wine name, the district or *appellation*, the wine region. On the next line I put my personal star-rating (in red), the name of the grower or producer, and when I thought it would be mature. My star system ran as follows: one star was a perfectly adequate wine, and if a customer asked me for it, I would be happy to get it for him. Two stars had quality, and was worth considering for listing, all things being equal (especially price!). Three stars was a wine that I would dearly love to buy for myself, if I could only afford it.

The rest of the front of the card was available for tasting notes, with the date of tasting on the left. When I tasted the same wine several times at intervals, these notes – one under the other – gave me an idea how the wine was changing as it matured.

DEDUCTIVE TASTING NOTATION

Like most tasters, I had written my tasting notes following the sequence of traditional headings: Appearance, Nose, Taste, Remarks. There is, however, a tendency to feel obliged to write something under each of these headings, regardless of importance. I noticed this particularly when I was in charge of the education course for those studying for the Master of Wine examination. Many of the students seemed to be wasting valuable time (which is of the essence in the exam) following the traditional tasting patterns. Therefore, to break the mould and force new thinking, I made them turn the page sideways, draw a line down the middle, and head the left-hand column 'Perceptions', and the right-hand column 'Deductions'. They were not allowed to write anything about the wine in the left-hand column unless they could match it with a logical correlation in the right-hand side. So it might be illuminating to go back to some of our tasting exercises, and rewrite notes in this pattern.

TIME-SCALE RECORDS

I have earlier mentioned how I found it helpful to note on my record cards the period when I guessed that the wine might be at its best. I noted this in the usual form, of pairs of years (e.g. 1987–1996 or 1990–2001). But I later found that people took it in better if it was expressed in graphical form. I got the idea from Renato Ratti, the great authority on the red wines of Barolo, who indicated their evolution with a chart of an upward slope of eight years while they are maturing, a plateau of eight years when they are likely to be at their best, and a downward slope of eight years when they might be in decline.

My maturity graphs showed dots during the years when the wine was not yet really drinkable, asterisks during its expected period of maturity, and then more dots during the years when it might be in decline, but still drinkable. So two wines might look like this:

```
1987–1996   · · · * * * * * * * * * * · · ·
1990–2001       · · · · * * * * * * * * * * * * · · · ·
```

COMPUTERIZING

I have yet to work out a simple way of keeping tasting notes on a computer. Ideally, one should be able to use the computer memory for compare/contrast recalls. Maybe one should evolve an essential 'key-words' programme for it. But apart from the vital word 'balance', I have yet to decide where I would put my priorities.

I have however found that a computer spreadsheet is a convenient way of recording time-scale data about wines. Each of the starting and finishing maturity dates (e.g. 1985 to 1996) must be placed in a separate column. One can then use the 'arrange/sort' program to print out, sequentially, either a 'ready by . . .' list of wines, or else a 'best before . . .' list.

I put the wine district, wine name, and vintage in separate columns, and also my star-rating of each wine in yet another column. Hence the computer can sort the wines out in a variety of ways. But I still have to make all the decisions.

Wine-tasting is human, and computers are machines; maybe tasting notes and tasting memories do not really belong in them.

SCORE-CARDS

If you should be asked to take part in a tasting panel, you might be required to use a score-card. A number of these have become hallowed by use, such as the DLG (German) scoring system, the INAO (French) procedures, and the Davis (American) 20-point system. By allotting points to named characteristics, they ought to ensure that all members of a panel are 'singing from the same hymn-sheet'. But by giving numerical 'weightings' to particular aspects of wine, they may tend to favour certain styles, or even give highest scores to 'blockbusters', at the expense of elegance and subtlety. If however you are tasting for yourself, you must be sure you know what you like, and give that the highest scores.

32
Farewell

The way that a wine can linger on the palate after the wine has been swallowed is sometimes called the wine's 'farewell'. What better way to end our series of tastings than by remembering all the good perceptions that have come our way?

33
Envoi

Wine-tasting is a many-faceted and multi-layered activity. It starts with the interplay between vine and soil and subsoil, and Man's influence on these and their ecology. These may be considered as Animal, Vegetable and Mineral, complicated (in due course) by pests and diseases, treatments and finings. Energy comes into the equation, with light and heat.

Vine-growing and wine-making involve inorganic and organic chemistry, and bring in the states of matter: solid, liquid and gas. Here again energy may be created and dissipated. Classical chemistry requires us to consider what is occurring at molecular level, but when we look at the acidities and tannins involved, we have to regard the electrical charges and potentials, and even to think in atomic and subatomic terms.

We may need to consider whether the same things happen in the mass, or at the interfaces; if an altered sequence of events might influence the outcome; and the time-scales along which things can happen.

We are dealing with stimuli and perceptions, and how they can vary throughout a population. We have to recognize that a human can respond to a wine physically, emotionally and intellectually. And that responses may be conditioned by past experiences, current physical state and evolving fashions.

More than a half-century of tasting has resigned me to learning about two vintages a year – North and South – from an increasing number of production areas. I acknowledge that it may well be impossible, yet I go on trying.

Werd' ich zum Augenblicke sagen:
Verveile doch! du bist so schön!
Dann magst du mich in Fesseln schlagen,
Dann will ich gern zu Grunde gehn!
(Goethe, Faust, Part I)

(If I should say, of a moment in time, 'Stay, you are so lovely', then you may bind me in chains, then I would gladly go down to the depths.'

With so many diverse factors in the world of wine, I am often tempted to echo the Elizabethan dramatist, saying: 'a Mad World, my Masters.'

Acknowledgements

Half a century in the wine trade has allowed me to learn much from the many people I have worked with, so I would like to thank them all collectively, and only mention by name a few from whom I have absorbed – almost by osmosis – some of the ideas put forward in this book. When you work and taste alongside people, you so often accept their views and learn from them, but otherwise, if you disagree, you then have to justify your opinion, which concentrates the mind and clarifies the thinking.

In Bordeaux, my French cousin, Frank Dunk, showed me how a professional wine-buyer approaches his job; and I managed to attend a number of Professor Jean Ribéreau-Gayon's evening lectures. Later on, Roger Danglade helped me to gain a more detailed knowledge of St Emilion, Pomerol and Fronsac châteaux. I gratefully went on a Bourse de Voyage to Champagne, after attending the Wine Trade Club's lectures in London.

In Burgundy, my chief mentors were Louis Vallet and Albert Pochon in the Côte-d'Or, Georges Burrier (for white wines), Pierre Malbec and Jules Chauvet (for red wines) in South Burgundy, and Michel Rémon in Chablis. In the Middle Loire, it was J. Touchais and his family, and Jacques Foucher in the Upper Loire.

For German wines, eighteen years working with the Hallgarten family allowed me to contrast Fritz Hallgarten's analytical tasting technique with his brother Otto's very down-to-earth approach, while Peter Hallgarten's training as a chemist specialising in sulphur compounds may explain my fixation with mercaptans.

In the Rhône valley, working with Marcel Bichat and Baron Le Roy de Boiseaumarié let me learn about the early days of the French *appellation contrôlée* system, and how it may have helped the region to improve its quality, its image and its economic viability.

In Italy, Dr Sappa, of Cuneo, took time off to guide my tastings of the wines of Piedmont, showing me how the best growers could bring out the '*terroir*' characteristics in their wines, and how nature and history had influenced the gastronomy of the region. Dr Renato Ratti gave me background information about the geological influences in the Barolo/Barbaresco region. The Rusca family, of Fara, taught me about the wines of the Novara hills.

I must indeed record my gratitude to colleagues in the Institute of Masters of Wine who helped me study and pass the examination, because it obliged me to work hard at my tasting, and so organize my thinking that I seem to have been able to learn much more *since* the exam.

My many friends and colleagues on the Technical Committees of BSI and ISO for Sensory Analysis let me see how tasting has been applied scientifically to other kinds of food and drink, and patiently tolerated, for twenty years, my unscientific approach to the subject. You may see how much I have picked their brains.

Some of the graphs and tables that I have used were drawn from the Swiss textbook by Benvegnin, Capt and Piguet, and have previously appeared in my chapter on wine in the *Food Industries Handbook*, 24th edition. Others are based on figures from *The Wine and Spirit Trade Diary* of 1968.

The shape of this book has been changed out of all recognition by Julian Jeffs's skilled and patient editing; I must accept responsibility for any remaining awkwardnesses and errors.

My love and thanks go to a highly supportive family during the writing of this book, and to my parents and wine-loving ancestors, from whom I may quite possibly have gained useful genes for my chosen career.

Short Bibliography

L'Amministrazione Provinciale di Cuneo, *La Vite ed il Vino nella Provincia Granda Cuneo*, 1974

Asociacion Nacional de Ingenieros Agronomos, *Boletin – Jerex Xérès Sherry*, Madrid: ANIA, 1958

Benvegnin, Lucien; Capt, Emile; Piguet, Gustave, *Traité de Vinification* (2e Edition), Lausanne: Librairie Payot, 1951

Bullen, A. H., ed., *Lyrics from the Dramatists of the Elizabethan Age*, London: John C. Nimmo, 1889

British Standards Institution Technical Committee on Sensory Analysis, London: BSI Sales & Customer Services, Publications

BS 5098 (1992), Glossary of terms relating to sensory analysis (ISO 5492)

BS 5586: Part 1 (1978), Specification for wine-tasting glass (ISO 3591)

BS 5929: Methods for sensory analysis of food: Part 1 (1986), General Guide to Methodology (ISO 6658); Part 4 (1986), Flavour profile methods (ISO 6654); Part 7 (1992), Investigating sensitivity to taste (ISO 3972); Part 9 (1992), Initiation and training of assessors in the detection and recognition of odours (ISO 8589)

BS 7667: Assessors for sensory analysis: Part 1 (1993), Guide to the selection, training and monitoring of selected assessors (ISO 8586 part 1); Part 2 (1994), Guide to the selection, training and monitoring of experts (ISO 8586 part 2).

Broadbent, Michael, *Wine Tasting*, London: Mitchell Beazley, 1982

Cocks, Charles, and Feret, Edouard, *Bordeaux et ses Vins* (11th Edition), Bordeaux: Feret, 1949

Cossart, Noel, *Madeira – The Island Vineyard*, London: Christie's Wine Publications, 1984

Dunne, John William, *An Experiment with Time*, London: A & C Black, 1927

Forbes, Patrick, *Champagne: The Wine, the Land and the People*, London: Victor Gollancz, 1967

Galet, Pierre, *Cépages et Vignobles de France*, Montpellier: Imprimerie du Paysan du Midi, 1962

Galet, Pierre, *A Practical Ampelography: Grapevine Identification*, trans. Lucie T. Morton, Ithaka, NY: Comstock Publishing Associates (first published as *Précis d'ampélographie pratique*), 1979

George, Rosemary, *Guide to Choosing Wine*, London: Bloomsbury, 1993

Gonzalez Gordon, Manuel Maria, Marqués de Bonanza, *Jerez – Xerez – Sherish* (3e Edition), Jerez-de-la-Frontera: Graficas del Exportador, 1970

Hallgarten, Siegfried Fritz, *Alsace and its Wine Gardens*, London: André Deutsch, 1957

Hanson, Anthony, *Burgundy*, London: Faber and Faber, 1982

Jeffs, Julian, *Sherry* (4th edition) London: Faber and Faber, 1992

Lagrange, André, *Moi, je suis vigneron*, Villefranche-en-Beaujolais: Les Editions du Cuvier, Jean Guillermet, 1960

Littré, E., *Dictionnaire de la Langue Française*, Paris: Librairie Hachette & Cie, 1873/4

Pemartín, Julian, *Diccionario del Vino de Jerez*, Barcelona: Editorial Gustavo Gili, 1965

Quittanson, Charles, Ciais, Adrien, and Vanhoutte, René (1949) *La Protection des Appellations d'Origine des Vins et Eaux-de-Vie et le Commerce des Vins*, Montpellier: La Journée Vinicole, 1949

Ribéreau-Gayon, Jean, *Traité d'Oenologie, transformations et traitements des vins*, Paris: Béranger, 1949

Robinson, Jancis, *Masterglass: A Practical Course in Tasting Wine*, London: Pan, 1983

– *Vintage Time-charts: Pedigree and Performance of Fine Wines to the Year 2000*, London: Mitchell Beazley, 1989

Roncarati, Bruno, *D.O.C.: The New Image for Italian Wines*, London, 1971

Simon, André Louis, *A Dictionary of Wine*, London: Cassell, 1935

Simon, André Louis, and Hallgarten, Siegfried Fritz, *The Great Wines of Germany*, London: McGraw-Hill, 1963

Sutcliffe, Serena, *The Wine Drinker's Handbook*, London: Pan, 1985

Syndicat des Vignerons des Costières du Gard, *Les Vins des Costières du Gard*, Nîmes, 1972

Vandyke Price, Pamela, *Enjoying Wine: A Taster's Companion*, London: Heinemann, 1982

Vedel, André, Charle, Gaston, Charnay, Pierre, and Tourmeau, Jules, *Essai sur la Dégustation des Vins*, Mâcon: S.E.I.V., 1972

The Institute of Masters of Wine Library is lodged with the Guildhall Library in the City of London. It includes a number of important collections of works on wine and related subjects, and is being re-catalogued.

Glossary

à la volée – the original disgorging method, flying the first champagne cork and attendant deposit, by swinging the bottle from neck down to neck up. (Replaced by the process of freezing the bottleneck.)

acéscence – the volatile acidity (*qv*) note on the nose.

acetic acid – weak acid found in plant juices and in vinegar: CH_3COOH.

acetobacter – a micro-organism that can turn wine into vinegar.

acid – substance which, when dissolved, releases hydrogen ions.

acidity – sharpness or sourness of taste. The *amount* of acidity is traditionally measured by the amount of alkalinity needed to neutralise it, when an indicator (*qv*) changes colour; the *strength* of the acidity is denoted by the pH (*qv*), which is the logarithm of the reciprocal of the hydrogen-ion concentration. It can be measured electrically.

acrid – sharp or biting to the taste; a pungent note.

acuity – physical keenness of perception.

adsorbtion – removal of unwanted particles or substances in a wine by attracting them on to the surface of a fining or filter.

agueusia – physical inability to taste.

albumen – the typical protein of egg-white.

alcohol – an important compound, present in wine; ethyl alcohol has the formula C_2H_5OH.

aldehydes – chemicals derived from alcohols by the loss of two hydrogen atoms (through oxidation creating a water molecule).

alkali – a base which is soluble in water, producing hydroxyl ions; capable of neutralising acids (*qv*).

ambience – the influence of the surroundings.

amphora – classical pottery wine-storage vessel with two handles.

anosmia – physical inability to smell things.

anthocyanins – colouring matter in the skins of grapes; colour tannins.

anti-oxidant – substance which inhibits or retards oxidation.

appellation – the official name of a wine (or other product), based on its geographical origin and method of production.

aqua regia – a mixture of acids (1 part concentrated nitric and 3 parts concentrated hydrochloric) used by alchemists to dissolve gold.

assemblage – putting *vitis vinifera* wines together. (See *coupage*.)

assessor – a sensory analyst (or taster) defined by ISO and BSI (*qv*).

aszu – the overripe and shrivelled Tokaji grapes, and the concentrated juice pressed out of them which is then added, in *puttonos*, to ordinary must, to make *tokaji aszu*.

attack – the first impression on the senses.

Ausbruch – the former Austro-Hungarian term for *aszu* (see above).

autolysis – chemical breaking-down of cells without outside stimulus.

auto-oxidation – oxidation which occurs without external oxygen, as a result of chemical changes.

bankers – in a blind tasting, wines which are immediately identifiable.

barrique – the Bordeaux term for the 225-litre hogshead cask.

Baumé – scale of density, used for measuring sugar content, named after Antoine Baumé (1728–1804). (See Table 1.)

Beerenauslese – harvesting by selecting individual grapes from the bunches.

benchmark – a standard of quality against which other wines may be judged.

bias – past experience or ideas tending to influence current tasting.

bison-grass – the herb used to flavour Zubrovka wódka.

bitter – one of the basic tastes; acrid or biting.

bi-valent – a compound which combines either with two

monovalent, or one bivalent, element or radical; for example ferrous iron Fe^{++}.

bland – with no outstanding sensory features.

blending – mixing wines together to achieve a desired style; the French distinguish between *assemblage* and *coupage*.

botanicals – natural flavourings, in particular those added before the second distillation of gin.

Botrytis cinerea – the grey mould which can also create noble rot (*qv*).

bottle-stink – a temporary (reductive) fault in old bottles, usually rectified by decanting or letting the wine breathe (take up oxygen) in the glass.

bouquet – a flowery aspect of the nose of a wine; develops in the bottle.

branded cork – a wine stopper with information (origin and/or vintage) burnt or otherwise printed on it.

Brix – scale of density used in the USA. (See Table 1.)

brut – relatively unsweetened, usually referring to champagne or other sparkling wine. (See also *dosage*.)

BSI – the British Standards Institution, producing various standard specifications for Britain, including sensory analysis standards. (See also ISO.)

bungs – the stoppers used at the tops of casks.

burette – a graduated glass dropper-tube with a tap at the bottom.

butts – largish wooden casks, usually referring to sherry containers.

calcareous – soil containing lime or chalk.

calories – units of heat, often used to indicate energy levels.

Canteiros – traditionally, madeiras that have not been *estufado* (*qv*).

cap – the mass of pips, skins, pulp (and sometimes stalks) that rises towards the surface during fermentation. (See *chapeau*.)

capsaicin – an alkaloid ($C_{18}H_{27}O_3N$) in (red) peppers giving a burning sensation.

cassis – the blackcurrant, and the Burgundian liqueur made from it.

catrame – the tarry sensory note imparted to the nebbiolo grape by certain Piedmont Italian soils.

cave – traditional wine-cellar, usually underground.

centrifuging – clarifying wine by spinning it so that solids are thrown to the sides.

cépage – the vine variety.

chapeau – the mass of pips, skins, pulp (and sometimes stalks) that rises towards the surface during fermentation. (See cap.)

chaptalisation – the adding of cane or beet sugar (or rectified grape-juice) to wine musts before fermentation in order to increase alcohol.

charmat – a method, named after its French originator, of inducing secondary fermentation in sparkling wines in large volumes. (See also *cuve close*.)

church windows – the tear-drops or flowlines on the sides of the glass after swirling it around.

clarifying – clearing a young wine of clouding particles, by introducing organic or inorganic finings (*qv*) which can adsorb them and carry them down into the lees.

clone – a distinct separate form within a vine-variety.

colloid – a substance like jelly or glue, which, when dissolved, will pass through a membrane; a state of subdivision of matter in which the particles are of ultramicroscopic size.

complexing – the development of aromas and flavours from primary to secondary and tertiary, as wines mature, due to chemical and structural changes.

contre-maître – assistant cellar-master.

corked/corkiness – wine-fault from an infection in the bark of the cork-oak from which the stopper was cut, giving a sensation on the nose like the smell of dry rot, and a parching sensation on the palate. (See also TCA.)

coupage – putting *vitis vinifera* wines together with wines from American vines, or from hybrids. (See *assemblage*.)

coupe – a shallow-bowled wineglass, which has been popular for serving Champagne.

crayère – Champagne wine-cellar hewn from the chalk.

cream of tartar – potassium bitartrate ($KHC_4H_4O_6$).

crème de tête – wine made from free-run (i.e., unpressed) grape-juice.

cryptogamic – referring to microscopic plants (and also ferns, lichens and mosses) with concealed fructification; particularly the moulds and other diseases affecting the vine.

cuvaison – the period of time that a wine is vatted (in a *cuve* or cask) during fermentation, usually to extract colour.

cuve close – the closed vat, usually insulated and able to resist pressure, used to make popular sparkling wines. (See *charmat*.)

Daltonism – colourblindness.

desiccation – the removal of moisture; the shrivelling and partial drying of grapes attacked by noble rot (*qv*).

dextrins – carbohydrates ($C_6H_{10}O_5$), in differing degrees of polymerisation, intermediate in character between sugars and starches, soluble in water and dilute alcohol.

dextrose – dextro-rotary glucose/sugar, bending polarised light to the right; also called glucose ($C_6H_{12}O_6$).

diatomaceous earth – filter-aid made from the flinty skeletal remains of diatoms, minute single-celled algae.

disgorging – uncorking and emptying wine-bottles, particularly after secondary fermentation of sparkling wines. (See *à la volée*.)

dosage – after disgorging (see above), the quantity of liquid (usually cane sugar dissolved in wine, with or without additional brandy) which is added before recorking with the final cork.

dry extract – the organic and inorganic components of a wine's 'body' that can be measured by evaporating the liquid part of a measured sample, and weighing the residue.

dry ice – solid carbon dioxide.

dry residue – see dry extract, above.

dulces – sherries of concentrated sweetness, for blending with dry sherries to sweeten them. (See *Vinos dulces*.)

Edelfäule – noble rot due to the action of *Botrytis cinerea* on ripe grapes.

electrolyte – a compound which may be decomposed by an electric current; the liquid in a cell.

élévage sur lie – maturing the wine on the primary lees.

El Niño – weather conditions resulting from reversal of regular currents in the Pacific.

enzyme – the active principle of a ferment.

erbace – a grassy character, often associated with Cabernet franc wines.

esterification – development of secondary (or tertiary) aromas due to interaction between alcohols and acids.

estufado – wine stored in a heated madeira cellar for a minimum of three months.

extract – see dry extract.

farewell – the final sensations left in the mouth by a wine.

febrifuge – a substance which reduces the body's temperature or fever.

fermentation – chemical change by the agency of enzymes (*qv*) resulting in the formation of alcohols and carbon dioxide gas.

ferric – the tri-valent (*qv*) form of iron Fe^{+++}.

ferrous – the bi-valent (*qv*) form of iron Fe^{++}.

feuillette – a Burgundian half-hogshead (about 112 litres).

filter aid – a substance introduced to fill the interstices of filter cloths, mesh, pads or sheets, and thus remove smaller-sized particles. (See diatomaceous earth.)

filtration – removing unwanted substances by passing the wine through a fine mesh or membrane.

finage – the South Burgundy word for an individual vineyard site.

fining – introducing an organic or inorganic substance in to the wine, which does not remain in it, but removes unwanted substances and clarifies it.

fino – sherry in a reductive state due to *flor* (*qv*).

flabby – a wine without structure, usually lacking acidity.

floating cap – fermentation where the cap (*qv*) is allowed to rise to the surface.

flocculation – coalescing and adhering into flake-like particles.

flor – the film yeast on the surface of a sherry.

flute – narrow-bowled glass, suitable for Champagne or sparkling wine.

foin coupé – the aroma of new-mown hay.

fortified – a wine with added alcohol.

foudre – a large wooden cask.

fraudeurs – wine cheats, often using unapproved procedures.

frizzante – containing dissolved carbon dioxide gas, so that it is half-sparkling.

Frostgeschmack – acrid taste due to frost action on unripe grapes.

fructose – laevulose or fruit-sugar, bending polarised light to the left.

fruit – a primary aroma and flavour, recalling a variety of fruits, not necessarily grapes.

full – a Gestalt sensation, whereby the body of the wine seems to fill the mouth.

fund de buto – traditional Italian phrase for wine left in the bottom of a bottle, for special enjoyment the following day.

furriness – a mouth-feel sensation on the inside of the mouth.

fusel oil – a deleterious product of distillation (fermentation amyl alcohol), requiring rectification, adsorbtion, or long maturing for elimination.

gallo-tannins – wood tannins, traditionally introduced into wine from the casks; more recently due to wood chips, wood powder, etc. (See oeno-tannins.)

gamay rouge à jus blanc – typical Beaujolais red-skinned grape with white juice, in contrast to the red-juiced Gamay fréaux.

gamut of aromas – concept of a scale of aromas, ranging from low notes to high notes.

gelatine – semi-solid semi-transparent colloidal substance, from bones, horns and hoofs, or from Irish moss seaweed.

Gestalt psychology – the study of how the mind responds to shapes and forms.

glucose – dextro-rotary sugar. See dextrose.

glycerine/glycerol $(CH_2OH)_2CHOH$ – a sweet-tasting viscid colourless liquid; a byproduct of fermentation of sugar into alcohol.

glycoside – a chemical whose molecule contains one or more sugars.

grand vin – the top wine of a reputed estate or area.

grassy – see *erbace* above.

green harvest – thinning-out the number of bunches on the vines before the harvest, to enhance the maturity and extract of the remainder.

gris de gris – rosé wine made from pink grapes.

grittiness – a mouth-feel sensation, possibly due to tannin flocculation in the mouth.

gros rouge – ordinary red wine, typical of the *pinard* wine rations of the French armies.

haze – slight cloudiness in a wine.

heady (*capiteux*) – with the alcohol giving a lift to the wine.

higher notes – see gamut of aromas.

hock – traditional English name for German rhinewines.

hogshead – wooden cask of about 225 to 250 litres content.

Humboldt current – cold sea-current from the southern polar regions of the eastern Pacific, particularly affecting the Chilean climate.

hybrid – a vine variety produced by crossing a *vitis vinifera* variety with an American vine variety.

imaginative tasting – recalling sensory impressions, and using them to compose juxtapositions, comparisons and contrasts.

indicator – a chemical which changes colour according to acidity or alkalinity.

inert gas – a gas which does not readily enter into a combination with other chemicals.

infusorial earth – a silicaceous deposit formed of fossil diatoms. (See diatomaceous earth.)

isinglass – finings substance derived from air-bladders of fish.

invert sugar – approximately 50 per cent dextrose and 50 per cent levulose obtained by the acid hydrolysis of cane sugar.

ISO – the International Standards Organisation, co-ordinating standards for Sensory Analysis.

iso-electric point – the point of electric neutrality; the pH value at which a substance (protein, etc.) is neutral. At a lower or higher pH value it acts either as a base or acid, respectively. Coagulation of colloids occurs at or near the isoelectric point.

Jahrgang – year of the vintage.

Kabinett – the first category of QmP (*qv*) German wines.

keeping potential – judgement about the length of time a wine may continue to improve.

lactic acid ($CH_3CH(OH)COOH$) – sour milk acid.

lactobacillus – micro-organism producing the malo-lactic fermentation (*qv*).

laevo-rotary – bending polarised light to the left (as in fructose).

laevulose – the Latin name for fructose (levulose) sugar (*qv*).

La Niña – secondary effect of *El Niño* reversal of currents in the Pacific.

lees – deposits at the bottom of casks or vats.

length of finish – the time that the flavours continue in the mouth, before after-taste begins.

lieu-dit – an individually-named vineyard site.

Limousin – the region around Limoges, in France.

maceration – contact between skins and juice during the wine-making process.

macération carbonique – fermentation procedure with the bunches of grapes surrounded with carbon dioxide gas.

malic acid ($HOOC.CH(OH).CH_2.COOH$) – the typical sour-apple organic acid.

malo-lactic fermentation – secondary fermentation by lactobacilli, turning the sharp malic acid into milder lactic (milk) acid.

masking – when a sensory note is obscured by a stronger note.

meniscus – the upwards curve of the wine against the sides of the glass.

mercaptans – sulphur derivatives, generally created by the action of yeasts on sulphur dioxide; contain the radical -SH.

metabolism – the process by which the body derives nutriment from food and other substances.

mezze – Mediterranean-type *hors-d'oeuvres*.

millésime – the year of the wine-harvest.

mistela – a wine in which the fermentation is arrested by the addition of alcohol before it is complete.

molecule – a group of atoms in a chemical union, forming the smallest particle of the substance.

monosodium glutamate ($HOOC.CH(NH_2)CH_2CH_2COONa$) – a flavour-enhancing substance, known shortly as MSG.

mould – filamentary fungoid growth.

mousse – the frequency and size of bubbles in a sparkling wine.

must – unfermented grape-juice for wine-making.

mycelia – the connecting threads of a mould or fungus.

naïve assessors – tasters who have not previously been on a tasting panel; members of the public in a marketing survey.

neutral alcohol – alcohol that has been rectified to remove flavour congeners.

noble rot – the effect of *Botrytis cinerea* on mature grapes. (See *pourriture noble* and *Edelfäule*.)

Oechsle – a scale of concentration, obtained by subtracting 1 from the specific gravity, then multipling by 1000. (See Table 1.)

oeno-tannins – grape tannins (anthocyanins), as contrasted with gallo-tannins (*qv*) from casks and vats.

orbits of electrons – the concept that charged particles circulate round the nucleus of the atom, similar to the paths of planets round the sun.

organic acids – natural acids found for example in grape-juice, as contrasted with inorganic acids.

oxidation – the action of oxygen on a chemical, as contrasted with the reductive state, where the concentration of hydrogen ions (pH) may inhibit the action of the oxygen.

passito – wine made from air-dried grapes.

pasteurisation – killing-off micro-organisms by the rapid application of heat and then cooling; named after Louis Pasteur.

Pavlovian effect – conditioned reflex causing automatic response.

perception threshold – the lowest concentration of a sensory note, when you are aware that it is there, but cannot identify its character or origin.

pétillant – semi-sparkling.

phosphorilisation – a stage in the fermentation process (which may become repetitive in cool and slow fermentations) with glycerine as its byproduct.

photosynthesis – a green plant's way of using sunlight to create chemical compounds.

phylloxera vastatrix – the vine-louse, with a complicated life-cycle, most devastating in its root-sucking form.

pièce – the Burgundian hogshead, of 215 to 225 litres.

pied de cuve – starting a small quantity of must into fermentation, before filling up the vat with more must.

pinard – French army slang for the red-wine ration.

Pineau des Charentes – a mistela (*qv*) made by adding cognac to Charentes grape-juice.

plant droit – a Pinot noir clone, with erect-growing shoots.

polarised light – light passed through a filter, so that it vibrates in only one plane.

polypeptides – compounds of two or more amino acids.

potentiometer – an instrument to measure electrical potential (charges).

pourriture noble – the noble rot, from the action of *Botrytis cinerea* on fully-mature grapes.

pre-phylloxera vines – ungrafted vines, planted prior to the onset of phylloxera; sometimes used to indicate their ungrafted progeny.

primary fermentation – the first yeast fermentation of wine-making.

primary notes – the aroma of a young wine before complexing (*qv*).

protective colloids – the concept, advanced by Professor Jean Ribéreau-Gayon, that certain colloidal substances in wine could make the wine more stable.

pseudothermal effect – the sensory impression (irrespective of actual temperature) that certain chemicals can give of heat or cold.

ptyalin – the digestive enzyme, present in the saliva, which can transform starches into sugars.

punt – the concave bottom of a wine-bottle.

pupître – the slanting stand, with holes for the necks of bottles, used in the Champagne method for sparkling wines.

QbA – *Qualitätswein bestimmter Anbaugebiete*; quality wine from specific wine-growing district.

QmP – *Qualitätswein mit Prädikat*; quality wine with suffix.

quantum mechanics – a system relating the behaviour of electromagnetic waves and particles to quantums of energy.

quintal/*quintale* – still widely-used term for 100 kilos of grapes or 100 litres of wine.

racking – drawing a wine off its lees into a clean cask.

recioto – sweet *passito* (*qv*) Italian wine made from dried grapes in Verona; originally made from the ripest grapes on the shoulders (*recie*) of the bunch.

rectified grape juice – rectified concentrated must, a neutral sugary liquid used for increasing sugar levels in a must (and hence alcohol levels in the ensuing wine) in cases where the use of cane or beet sugar is forbidden.

remueurs – skilled workers who shake, twist and tilt bottles of sparkling wines in the *pupîtres* (*qv*) for the Champagne process.

residual sugar – sugar remaining in the wine after fermentation has stopped.

riparian – pertaining to the bank of a river.

rouse – to stir up the lees of a wine with a rousing-rod through the bunghole.

Saccharomyces ellipsoideus – typical wine-yeast.

saignée – 'bleeding' a vat by drawing off some of the juice, in order to improve the skins-to-juice ratio in watery vintages. The run-off juice is often used to make *rosés*.

sake – Japanese rice-wine, brewed with symbiotic action between a mould and a saccharomyces.

secondary fermentation – subsequent yeast fermentation, or malo-lactic fermentation.

sediment – solids deposited out of a wine, sometimes in cask (see lees), or more usually in bottle.

selected assessors – trained sensory analysts.

shape-words – descriptions relating to Gestalt concepts.

shooked – dismantled cask-staves bundled together with the hoops.

sorbate – a chemical that may be used to stabilise wines.

sorbus – the Mountain Ash tree and its fruit.

SO_2 – sulphur dioxide.

Spätlese/Spaetlese – wine made from late-gathered grapes.

specific gravity – relative weight, measured on a scale against distilled water, which has a value of 1000.

spritzig – slightly sparkling.

stomata – the breathing-pores of a plant, which appear as black transverse holes in a wine-cork.

submerged cap – fermentation where the cap (*qv*) is prevented from rising to the surface by a grid placed in the vat.

sucrose – cane or beet sugar.

sugar – carbohydrate with the formula $C_6H_{12}O_6$.

sulphur – yellow chemical element used in wine-making in various forms, usually as sulphur dioxide SO_2, as an anti-oxidant and against infections.

supermaturity/*surmaturation* – riper than commercial maturity.

supersaturated solution – a solution whose solute content is greater than normal and is prone to crystal formation.

supple/*souple* – a descriptive term, especially for red Bordeaux, suggesting an easy-drinking wine without excess acidity or tannin, yet with vigour, and certainly not flabby (*qv*).

suspension – particles floating in a liquid, too small or light to deposit.

Süssreserve – sterile-filtered grape juice kept back to sweeten fully fermented wine.

syllogism – a form of reasoning, consisting of three propositions: the first two are the premises, and the last the logical conclusion.

symbiosis – the relationship between two organisms, each of which is dependent on the other.

synergism – a state in which the sum of the whole appears more than the sum of the parts.

taint – an unwanted off-flavour or aroma.

tannin – the traditional way of describing the anthocyanins found in red wines (and in strong teas).

taste-vin – shallow silver or silver-plated tasting vessel, embossed and recessed to throw light on the wine-colour. (Sometimes referred to as a *tasse à vin*.)

tasting glass – wine glass with a stem and a foot (so that the hand does not obscure the view), curved walls so that the wine may be swirled around, and sufficient volume to allow aromas to develop.

tawny – brownish tint of lightish red, used to describe a wood-matured port.

TCA – 2,4,6 Trichloroanisole; now thought to be a factor in corkiness.

teinturier – a grape yielding red juice that is capable of imparting colour to a wine without skin maceration.

terroir – qualities of origin influencing the style of a wine, particularly soil, subsoil, aspect and microclimate, and their effect on the vine varieties.

threshold – a lower sensory limit. (See perception threshold.)

titration – volumetric analysis, by dropping a liquid from a burette (*qv*) until an indicator (*qv*) changes colour.

tonneau – a notional tun cask of Bordeaux wine, equivalent to four hogsheads (*barriques*) of 225 litres.

tri-valent – a compound with three valency bonds that combines with other elements or radicals, for example ferric iron (Fe^{+++}). (See ferric and bi-valent.)

trocken – dry fully-fermented German wine.

Trockenbeerenauslese – rich German wine made from over-ripe shrivelled grapes attacked by *Edelfäule* (*qv*).

troisième envinage – Burgundy casks which have already housed two vintages of lesser wines, and are now ready for the finer growths.

ullage – the airspace in a cask above the surface of the wine.

venturi tube – narrowing of a flow-line to create subsequent acceleration of flow and/or suction.

véraison – the change of colour of the grapes on the vine, from their initial green colour, to their subsequent colour; usually about 50 days after the flowering, and about 50 days before the vintage.

vieilles vignes – old vines, usually indicating a higher quality wine than the norm.

village wines – refers to intermediate quality Burgundies, with the village name such as Gevrey-Chambertin, better than generic Bourgogne, but ranked lower than site-named or grand vin (*qv*) Burgundies.

vin de paille – rich wine, made from grapes dried on straw mats.

Vin Jaune – special Jura wine, matured (like sherry) under a *flor* (*qv*) film.

vinification – the process of wine-making after the vintage.

vin ordinaire – straightforward wine for daily drinking.

vinos dulces – sherries of concentrated sweetness, for blending with dry sherries to sweeten them.

vinosity – development of secondary flavours of a 'winey' character.

vintage port – port of a single year which is bottled not more than two years after the vintage, and matured in bottle.

viscosity – stickiness or gumminess in a liquid which hinders or reduces its rate of flow through an aperture.

volatile acidity – abnormal amounts of acetic or vinegary acid, noticeable on the nose since it is 'volatile' and evaporates easily; abbreviated as VA.

weighting – allocation of importance among sensory attributes.

Weinlese – the German wine-harvest.

well-balanced – with all desirable attributes in harmony; without any overweening attribute.

Welschriesling – (*Wälschriesling, Laski Rizling, Vlassky Ryzling, Olasz Rizling, Riesling Italico*, Italic Riesling) a different white vine variety from the classic Rhineriesling, so named because the old German name for Italy was Welschland.

wine-press – cellar equipment used to squeeze must or wine from the grape skins, pulp and pips; in white wines it is normally used before fermentation; in red wines, after fermentation and maceration.

wódka – the Polish spelling of vodka, pronounced with a long 'o', as 'vood-ka'.

wood-chips/wood-powders – now used to 'oak' wines, as an alternative to cask-ageing.

zona de crianza – in Spanish wine law, where a wine is matured and developed.

zona de producción – in Spanish wine law, where the wine originated and was made.

Index
